CRACKING THE HEALER'S CODE

CRACKING THE HEALER'S CODE

A Prescription for Healing Racism
& Finding Wholeness

Milagros Phillips

NEW DEGREE PRESS

COPYRIGHT © 2021 MILAGROS PHILLIPS

Cover design Milagros Phillips

CRACKING THE HEALER'S CODE
A Prescription for Healing Racism & Finding Wholeness

ISBN

978-1-63730-338-2   *Paperback*
978-1-63730-339-9   *Kindle Ebook*
978-1-63730-340-5   *Digital Ebook*

I dedicate this book to our global family and to those who are ready to transform their racial conditioning.

CONTENTS

———

"The great solution to all human problems is individual inner transformation."

—VERNON HOWARD

ACKNOWLEDGMENTS

———

I want to start by thanking Eric Koester, whose genius idea it was to get college students to write a book in less than a year, and Kip Dooley, for suggesting I join the class to write this book. I also thank the editors and staff at New Degree Press for their great commitment to the process.

My sons, for tirelessly contributing time and energy and finding all the missing commas, grocery shopping, and preparing meals so I could continue to work on this book. And my daughter, who is one of my greatest cheerleaders!

My beta readers: Debbie Rosas, Ginny Baldwin, Jennifer Mathews, and Thaddeus Gamory. Thank you so much for the great feedback, questions, and early praise! Jennifer, thank you for all the edits and the great talks.

My campaign contributors, without whom this book would not be a reality. Thank you all so much!

A. Sebris, Abisola Pua Faison, Aja Davis, Alex Cary, Alfonso Sasieta, Alison Card, Alyssa Johnson, Amy Soucy, Amy Verebay, Andrea Nagel, Anjel B. Hartwell, Annie, Mike, and Avery Bukay, Barbra Esher, Betty, B. Pleasant, Brenda Yosseti Beza, Brenden McMullen, Brenna C. Frandsen, Caitlin Duffy, Candace Simpson, Carin Rockind, Carla, Celeste

Elliott, Charolette Letourneau, Chella Drew, Cherdikala, Cherie Mejia, Christie Jimenez, Christina Jett Kowalski, Christopher Dooley, Christy Dimson, Claudia Norby, Connie Duval, CVSongstress, Cynthia Harvey, Deirdre McGlynn, Dianne Shepherd, Donna Bohanon, Eleanor LeCain, Elizabeth Johnson, Elizabeth Santos, Eric Koester, Erin Bentley, F. G. Watkins, Frances Kao, Gail Cowan, Greta Janet, Gretchen Kainz, Grigg3, Heather Fogg, Heather Plucker, Ina A. Lukas, James S. Pfautz, Janice Eng, Jaq Belcher, Jawltn, Jazmin Hupp, Jean-Luc Dessables, Jennifer Booker, Jennifer Mathews, Jennifer Voss, Jonathan Rosenthal, Joseph Phillips, Julia Jarvis, Kaisha Lawrence, Kara Barnett, Karen Friedman, Kathleen Gille, Kathrine Weissner, Kathryn Bailey, Kay Randolph-Pollard, Kelli Campbell, Kenzie Raulin, Kevin Matta, Kris Miller, Kristi Plucker Kristiana Harapan, Lauren Boudreaux, Laurie M. McTeague, LaVerne Day, Lia Venet, Linda Newton, Lisa Peters, Lynne C. Davis, Mara Lee Gilbert, Mara Sobotka, Margaret Belland, Marta Valentin, Martha Creek, Mary Lynne, Meade Hanna, Megan, melissiab, Melody Eddy, Mercedes Eugenia, Michael King Jr., Michael Watts, Michele Sullivan, Michelle Hanson, Miriam Kaufman Nash, Nancy E. Shaw-Hart, Nicholette Routhier, Nicole Love, Patrice Dunckleyl, Peter Sklivas, Philip Arny, Rachel Darrow, Rebecca Beall, reldridge2020, Shadowwk, Shirani Pathak, Spring George, Stefania Dominguez, Stefanie Ziev, Susan Collin Marks, Susan Rios, Susan Sparkman, Tami Fairweather, Tara K. Gorman, Tarsha Burton, Tatyana Foltz, texasnyc, Thomas Douglass, Tina McRorie, Tohewlinl, Valerie Smith, Vergie Cooper, Will Rogers, Wilson Marykate, and Winalee Zeeb.

You are the reason I continue to do this work!

INTRODUCTION

A PRESCRIPTION FOR HEALING RACIAL CONDITIONING AND FINDING WHOLENESS

"Know what you stand for, for someday you may need to stand alone."
—FELICIANO (DON FELIPE) HUGHES WALTERS, MY FATHER

The day Dr. Martin Luther King, Jr. died, I locked myself in the bathroom and couldn't stop crying. I got my calling that day, at thirteen years old. My mother had gone to the grocery store, and my father and I were watching something on the television. The program was interrupted to announce Dr. King had died. I was devastated. My father knocked on the bathroom door, asking if I was all right. I just said, "Yes, I'm fine." But I wasn't fine.

While in the bathroom, I realized we had left our beautiful island to move to a country where they killed people for being Black. And as if that was not enough, I was losing my mind. While in the bathroom, I heard a voice that said, "You are to continue the work." This upset me even more. They had just killed a man for doing race work. There was no way I was ever going to do that.

Fast forward to 2020; more than fifty years had passed since Dr. Martin Luther King, Jr. was murdered. For decades, we had been seeing Black men killed by the police on our TV, more recently on social media. But this time, we were locked down in the middle of a pandemic, isolated from family, friends, and workmates. It was the early days of the pandemic. Many were considering the growing number of deaths from COVID-19 while alone in their homes, perhaps even pondering our mortality. We watched a man begging to be allowed to breathe, calling for his mother, and taking his last breath. Then, there before our very eyes, we watched him die. His name was George Floyd, and his murder, in Minneapolis, Minnesota, has changed everything when it comes to race in America and around the world. His last words, "I can't breathe," became the mantra as his death prompted protests around the US and the world.

This murder woke the world to the reality Black and Brown bodies are treated differently than White bodies in America. It woke the world to inequalities and inequities in ways nothing else had done up to that point, much the way I woke up when I was thirteen years old.

The years passed, I went on with my life, and I started to do personal development work. Then, one day, a friend who knew me to be a fan of Tony Robbins, the motivational speaker, told me he would be speaking in Boston, and she had a ticket for me to see him live. It was the mid-1980s, and I was still resisting doing race work. But something happened to me in that room of about one thousand people. As I looked up at Tony Robbins on stage, it occurred to me that I could do what he was doing, and I would do it with anything but race. I had already been speaking and training about such subjects as time management and sales—anything other than race. I knew I had to keep speaking about anything except race. But that would change.

A few years later, while attending college, I had to take a diversity class and write a thesis. The research opened my eyes to race and racism, and I have never looked back. While I trained to be an artist, and continued to paint, today I am a keynote speaker, TEDx presenter, three-time author (not counting this book), and certified coach. I specialize in creating a safe space for engaging in difficult conversations. I design strategic learning programs for clients seeking to enhance equity and inclusion (EI) by adding race literacy to their EI initiatives. I use history, science, research, and storytelling to create compelling, life-transforming experiences that lead to understanding. I have seen people do more than change their minds about race; I have seen them change their hearts. My calling is healing racism, but my passion is transformation. I have spent the last thirty years healing from internalized racial conditioning and helping others do the same. But it's not been the easiest path, especially in those early years.

Racism impacts everything, from education to transportation, from housing to salaries. But most insidious is the trauma that silently lives in our bones.

"Just keep moving forward" became my mantra. These were the words I kept telling myself to keep going all those years. By 2020, I had been doing healing racism work for a long time and had successfully guided thousands through my process. I was used to working with large numbers of participants in organizations, but getting the general public to attend workshops, become race literate, and understand the need for healing was more than a challenge. I had given up on the idea of having more than fifty people at a time receive information that would transform the way they interacted with race and racism.

But then George Floyd, a Black man, had been killed by a policeman. The video was there for all to see, and the world responded. I knew the world was traumatized, but I also knew it wasn't time to start the healing process.

On May 27, 2020, a friend who knew I had been doing healing racism work for years called me to say, "You must be really busy with all this racism stuff." She sounded rather frantic. "No," I responded. "It's not my time yet. People are in the thick of it. Most of them don't realize they've been traumatized. They are all still acting out of their stress response—fight, flight, or paralysis. They are not yet ready for healing. But they will be." Still, I wanted to do something to help with the initial pain because people just seemed lost.

On May 29, I decided to do a program to help people understand and move past the trauma they had experienced. I created a webinar called Trauma, Race, & Healing. I called a friend who had been helping me set up a podcast and I said, "I know it's Friday, but I want to offer this program on Monday as a lunchtime webinar." We created an announcement, put it on Facebook and my LinkedIn account, and sent it to my small mailing list. We were expecting our usual twenty, maybe even thirty. The announcements went out on Saturday. In the first two hours, we had seventy-five participants sign up for the program. We thought by Monday we might reach ninety or so.

When the time came to open the Zoom room to receive participants, we let in the first one hundred, and there were another one hundred in the waiting room. They were offering us money to let them into the session. Finally, we opened the session to admit all, and the following week, we had five hundred participants join the call. I was overwhelmed by the response, and I felt the tears welling up.

I was overcome with emotions! I had waited decades for people to wake up to the need for race literacy and healing. I had been inviting, asking, and sometimes begging people to attend my racial healing seminars. I was unprepared for what happened because, frankly, I had given up the idea people would ever wake up, at least not in my lifetime.

The feedback has been fantastic, and people report they are healing relationships not just with coworkers, but also with family members. It's transforming the way they feel about race. It's changing how they work on teams and the way they view themselves and their company. Moreover, it's giving them a new sense of freedom, it's making it easier to speak about race, and it's giving them a vision of a world of justice, compassion, and love.

I started this book more than eighteen years ago. I have written three books since I started this one. Writing this book seemed daunting to me. There are so many layers to it. The healing process alone has thirteen stages. In addition, there is a segment that breaks down the Spanish caste system. Another section covers how groups communicate through their racial filters and so much more.

I lived with a great deal of instability, even homelessness, a couple of times. But it was that very instability that made my work experiential. Walking through those difficult times taught me to do healing racism work with compassion and respect for all involved. Passing through the fire helped me to understand the structure of the system. Without that understanding, my work would be missing a valuable grounding in reality. There is no substitute for experience.

Finally, it's time. I'd like to begin by defining healing for the purpose of this book. Healing is about seeing, feeling, or awakening to what is not functioning right (dysfunction/malfunction) and is therefore causing pain (physical, mental, emotional, and spiritual). As a result, these imbalances wreak havoc on the body, family, community, country, and world. Healing is a pathway to wholeness.

So what is healing racism? Healing racism is transforming mind and heart to access the wholeness that lives behind the damage done in more than five hundred years of racial conditioning. It gives historical context and connects the past to the present. Healing racism takes people through the stages of healing, which requires awareness, connection, and action. It is a process that connects them to their authentic self, the self we hide from the world, or we may not even know is there. The part of the self that knows truth speaks from the heart and listens to the inner promptings.

Healing is moving from what is unhealthy, not working, out of order, or just plain wrong. It is about finding what's right; functioning relieves pain and causes health. It allows us to gain a new understanding by connecting the past to the present and finding a cure that stops the pain and brings about inner and outer peace.

Healing requires change. Conscious change requires courage. And allowing the new knowledge to guide us involves wisdom.

In healing, we seek knowledge. This is not to beat others over the head with it or to wag the finger of blame at them. In healing, we transform knowledge into wisdom. We use knowledge to know ourselves and the world better. We use knowledge to strengthen and empower ourselves. And ultimately, we allow that knowledge, combined with our wisdom, to lead us to inspired action.

Healing from racism requires information that leads to transformation, or what I call race literacy. *"Race literacy is the knowledge and awareness of the history of race, how one is acculturated into a racial caste, the systems in the nation-state that support race as a human divide, and the impact of all of the above on our current events and individual lives"* (11 *Reasons to Become Race Literate*, 2016).

Healing is about treating the whole being: mind, body, spirit, and emotions. Healing from racism is about creating a safe space that allows for tears and emotions to surface, as emotions need expression for healing to occur. Healing is for tending a five-hundred-year-old wound, opening it, cleaning it, and finally, perhaps for the first time, allowing it to heal!

Over the years, people have found the lesser-known history shared in my seminars invaluable to their healing. Makes sense! When you go to the doctor, they have you fill out a history form that includes what has ailed the people in your family. It is the same with healing racism. We need our history to understand what has come before that is causing the problem today. We also require our history to see when we are recreating the past. And we need to decipher the connection between the past and the present to create a different future.

In 2001, while I was living in Michigan, doing my Race Demystified program, the Fortune 100 company I worked with made the program mandatory for its leaders and managers. It was a two-day program, and I had structured the content to include history that was not readily available to the average American. For instance, back then, most people didn't know race riots in the early 1900s were characterized by White people destroying Black communities. The rioters would destroy or burn homes and offices, steal property, and kill Black citizens. Such was the burning of the Black section of Tulsa, Oklahoma, in 1924.

I was pretty open and naive when I first moved to Michigan. Then, as I do now, I would encourage participants to contact me with questions and comments after the two-day program. At that point, I had no idea Michigan had the highest number of KKK and neo-Nazis in the US. I was facilitating a program, and the evening of the first day, a young man in his early thirties, who shared he had been trained as a neo-Nazi from the time he was twelve during part of the program, called me at home. He said he had never heard any of the histories I had shared. He then apologized to me for all the horrible things he had done to Black people. He didn't go into detail, and I just listened.

On day two of the program, he took copious notes about the healing process, asked questions, and seemed really engaged. The program ended and I didn't hear from him again. Then, two months later, he called me. I had prepared a "train-the-trainer" program to prepare facilitators to continue the work for the Fortune 100 company where he worked. He asked if I would recommend him to be one of the trainers. He said throughout the last couple of months, what he had learned about race and racism was haunting him. He thought he could be an asset to his organization by sharing his story and becoming a trainer.

I recommended him, but the company had already chosen who would participate in the program. It was an opportunity lost for both him and the company. He had a unique history, one that could have been an asset, especially since others had received similar neo-Nazi training working for that company.

This man's heart had been touched, and I knew he would never be the same again. It's experiences like this and many others that have kept me going over the years.

Healing not only changes hearts and minds, but it also leads people to do the right thing, to speak out against what is wrong, and to make a difference right where they are, in their families, or their jobs. In 2012, while working on a project called Congressional Conversations on Race, a White congressman stood up during the sharing portion of the program and said, *"I had no idea how some of the laws we had made were hurting African-American families, and I want to do something about that."* He then pointed to several Republican members, as well as Democrats, and said, *"I'm going to set up a committee, and I want you to join me."*

In the decades I have spent doing this work, I find most people want to do the right thing, but they don't always know what to do. White people want to do something about racism and be good allies to People of Color, but they don't always know how. They don't see the oppression hidden behind privilege (access, opportunity, immunity, and innocence). They fail to see themselves as part of the problem, so they don't know how they can be part of the solution. Meanwhile, People of Color are missing vast segments of their history. Their significant contributions are missing from history books, making it difficult for them to connect the past to the present. They are not always aware of the intergenerational and historical trauma they carry in their bodies and its effect on their current lives. My desire is to bring a process with a twenty-year track record of success to the general population.

The 2020 election and the subsequent years are going to be packed with issues of race. From reparations to education, the race conversation is about to take center stage. But what about the much-needed conversation on healing? The racial divide is a five-hundred-year-old legacy, well established in our hemisphere, that affects all aspects of life and costs some their liberty and their lives. Yet, rarely do we address racism as something that needs healing. We are on the brink of a racial healing transformation. As of the writing of this book, 210 cities, counties, and state legislatures have declared racism a public health crisis.

Cracking the Healer's Code looks at a variety of modalities, philosophies, and patterns. It weaves a tapestry of ideas that create a holistic view of how the past connects to the present and the future. It asks us to breathe and be present with what is happening in our bodies to stay grounded while reading the book.

The book is divided into *two parts*. The first part of the book gives the *what*—what racism is, where it came from, what it developed out of, and how it affects us in mind, body, emotions, and spirit. Part two is *how* to heal it, transform it, and stay on the path to racial sobriety.

This book is experiential. It moves the reader through a process. As you read it, you will find that layers of misinformation, preconceived notions, and stereotypes we accept as truth will begin to fall away. You may encounter feelings, emotions, and body sensations you didn't know were there. As a result, you will be transformed, filled with realizations, and have a more profound sense of who you are. *Cracking the Healer's Code* invites you as the reader to take your place in the healing story. By understanding the connection between the five layers of racial conditioning (institutional, systemic, internalized, personal, and interpersonal) and walking through the healing process, you will be transformed.

This book contains the thirteen stages of healing that make up the Healer's Code. You will experience the stages in four parts:

1. **Awakening** – Coming out of the sleep induced by centuries of misinformation. We get angry at being awakened and often want to go back to sleep.

2. **Grieving** – We grieve when we awaken to a new reality. We realize the world is not what we thought it was. We experience our loss of innocence. We grieve that loss, and at times, we want to go back to sleep.

3. **Healing** – Healing is the process that leads to wholeness and is characterized by the thirteen stages. Each stage is detailed to make it easy to find where you are in the process of healing.

4. **Becoming Empowered** – This is where we begin to live with the awareness of who we really are, our true nature. Wholeness allows us to be comfortable in our skin and bring our best selves to everything we do. Wholeness is about being complete and knowing we are enough!

This book contains quotes by people whose names may be known to you, along with quotes from people who are famous to me, the words of my ancestors. These are the words that drive my life and sustain this work. In them, may you find the words of your ancestors to give you courage on your journey of healing.

These pages invite you to take your new learning and use it to create a world where you consider the impact of race on your actions, reactions, and interactions, as it challenges you to look at race in your own life, regardless of the color of their skin. Further, the book challenges you to consider, that while racism is a problem *for* People of Color, it is not the problem *of* People of Color; therefore, People of Color cannot solve racism. *Cracking the Healer's Code* walks you through the stages of healing and invites you to apply the stages to your life, organizations, and communities. It is an invitation to take your rightful place in the human family, to create a vision of a more equitable future, and then work toward that vision.

It's been more than fifty years since the civil rights movement, yet America still struggles with issues of race. It impacts every segment of American life, from health care to education, from housing to employment, and our judicial system. Race is one of those topics Americans prefer would just go away, disappear from the national discourse, and stop pestering us into taking a long, hard look at how race has impacted and continues to impact our lives, regardless of the color of our skin. We resist the education that can lead to transformation. We forget what we resist persists. If we are going to transform our nation, we need to heal both individually and collectively.

QUESTIONS TO CONSIDER:

- What drew you to this book?

- What do you hope to get out of it?

PART 1

A DEEPER UNDERSTANDING

CHAPTER 1

PREPARING FOR
THE JOURNEY

———

"Sometimes the longest journey we make is the
sixteen inches from our heads to our hearts."

—ELENA AVILA

We cannot be forced to heal. Healing is something we come
to when life has thrown enough at us we have no choice but
to change. Healing is something we experience when we
are ready.

There is a hospital outside of Beijing, China, where the
patients are called students. These students, all diagnosed with
near terminal and terminal illnesses, are in this hospital for
months, sometimes a couple of years. Beyond a healthy diet and
exercise, the students learn about healing. The interesting thing
is they learn healing doesn't take long. Preparing to be healed,
accepting they can heal, and being able to trust they are healed
are what take time. *"The world's largest medicineless hospital,*
Huaxia Zhineng Qigong Center, was established by Grandmaster

Pang Ming, MD, to explore the human body science—the new
frontier of medicine. Over the years, the Center has treated more
than one hundred thousand patients with one hundred eighty
different diseases and achieved an overall success of 95 percent"
(101 *Miracles of Natural Healing*, Benefactor Press, VHS).

To prepare is to get ready. It is to set aside time to enter the experience with curiosity and humility.

To prepare to heal from racism, we need to understand we don't know what we don't know. There's a lot of missing information, and nothing is random. In healing from racism, the process is about putting new knowledge and awareness in the place of old ideas. It is about gaining information that helps us understand the conditions that led to internalize racial conditioning and gives us tools for transformation, healing, and accessing wholeness.

Life is a continuum, connecting one moment to the next, one era to the next, and one generation to all others. All humans are connected through one genetic line, making us one human family.

Preparation means entering the exploration of healing from racism with an open mind and an open heart. It means knowing we will make mistakes, none of us gets it right all of the time, and we need to be willing to be patient with ourselves and others. It means being self-caring, taking care of your body, mind, spirit, and emotions while caring for others. It means learning to open our hearts. It is about being willing to learn, change, and do things differently.

Preparation requires we be willing to delve into the shadow side of history and feel the emotions that arise. Healing engenders hope in the future, a belief that things can be better than they are, and knowing the journey is undoubtedly worth it.

You are preparing to enter into a healing process by reading this book. *Cracking the Healer's Code* is based on my two-day experiential intensive workshop, Race Demystified. 2021 commemorates the twentieth year I have offered this program.

To give you a sense of where we are healing, here are some experiences that participants have shared about this work over time.

The Race Demystified workshop moved me deeply on multiple levels—intellectual, emotional, somatic, and energetic. I'd already done a good deal of self-study, group study, and organized antiracism programming, but this was unique. I was struck by the depth and range of the work, how much it impacted and stayed with me, and how such deep results could be reached in such a short time. I believe that has everything to do with the embrace of emotional processing and compassion, which is important and often overlooked part of this work. For all of that, I am deeply grateful. Thank you, Milagros, for leading and modeling a truly effective way to move forward. —Kellee Educei, Participant, Race Demystified, Spring 2021

Nancy, a White woman, attended a two-day Race Demystified seminar and shared how those two days gave her the tools to change her relationship with her father:

I took your weekend workshop in New York City a few summers ago. I've used the material I learned through that, and then a few of these "lunch and learns" (weekly race literacy programs created to help the community heal) I've been able to attend the last year. It wasn't just one conversation; it was a lot of difficult conversations. But I was able to approach my dad in a new way—my entitled, Republican-for-life father. I was able to come in curiously to get to know the family secrets, like "What did your father believe?" "What did your grandfather believe?" I used everything you told me. There were times he cried. There were times I cried. But last Friday, he called me and told me he knew I should be the first to know he had officially changed his political party affiliation after the insurgency. He was so incensed about that! And we never could have even gotten to know each other and establish a friendship—we never had that before, ever! I couldn't have done it without your weekend workshop. So, thank you.

Family healing is part of the powerful process; healing our families ultimately heals the human family. As you read this book, family patterns that seem familiar but for which you have no explanation will be revealed.

Bernadette Pleasant, a Black woman from New Jersey and the founder of Femme! a somatic, emotional release experience, spoke when she attended my two-day Race Demystified program:

I am so excited to introduce you to Milagros Phillips. This woman offers a race training seminar, and I had the incredible opportunity of experiencing it before I went. I wondered what was there for me to learn. I mean, you know, I know what it's like to be Black in America. And I walked into this room and got such an education. It's a two-day seminar, and I'm so excited about it. I felt it was a responsibility to share this. It was all the things we started with an incredible history; I learned so many things. And we did exercises and all kinds of incredible learning, deep learning. But more than just learning the details, we learn what to do with it, and we were charged to do something! Like, how do you do this? It's like a new way of walking and learning and teaching. I really felt compelled to share. I tell you, in this racial climate, this is such an opportunity to come and learn and ask questions. It was incredible what happened in that room and what came up in that room. And so, I encourage you to get in that room.

Often African-Americans feel as Bernadette did, but there is so much we don't know about race in America. Opening ourselves to learning can be very healing. The best way to prepare for the journey is to come to this book as you are. As you read, you will receive what you need.

Preparing for the journey means staying open, receptive, and honest about your feelings. If you engage with this process, you will find you experience parts of yourself in new and compassionate ways. You will understand family patterns and behaviors that seemed strange and different. You may even see your ancestors in a whole new light.

To prepare, let yourself be present with your feelings as they arise, and remember to breathe. Being conditioned doesn't make you defective. If anything, it says you're a good learner, but you were badly taught.

CHAPTER 2

WHY IT HURTS

———

"The legal battle against segregation is won,
but the community battle goes on."

—DOROTHY DAY

There is nothing natural about segregation. Neurologically, we are wired to connect with others; mirror neurons in our brains are stimulated when we're interacting with other people. According to Matthew Lieberman, a professor and social cognitive neuroscience lab director at UCLA Department of Psychology, Psychiatry, and Biobehavioral Sciences, social pain is real, and human beings are wired for connection.

> *Over the past two decades, my colleagues and I have created a new kind of science called "social cognitive neuroscience." Using tools like functional magnetic resonance imaging (fMRI), we have made startling discoveries of how the human brain responds to social world—discoveries that were not possible before. These findings repeatedly reinforce the conclusion our brains are wired to connect with other people (Lieberman 2014).*

While we may be wired to connect, the ways in which we connect to one another does not always go well, and the body feels it.

The body makes a chemistry for everything—a look, a smell, a word. That chemistry can make us feel good, bad, or neutral. The microaggressions experienced by People of Color are real and affect their health. Microaggressions are acts of discrimination or discriminatory statements that are subtle and often unintended. Like when people say to a Black person, "I don't see you as Black." Or "You're so well-spoken," even though you're speaking your native language. Take the work environment. People of Color are often seen as less qualified, even though they attend the same colleges as White-bodied people and have to pass the same tests and get the same degree. Even when they do the same job as their White peers, they get paid less and are often left out of after-work social gatherings. We forget people hire, mentor, and promote for comfort.

White people leave People of Color out of social gatherings because they are uncomfortable—not just with People of Color, but with themselves. They feel if they invite a Person of Color, other White people in the group may feel uncomfortable, or they don't want to be left out of the next gathering. Some White people think they are being protective because they know some members of their group may make racist comments when they are together that they would not say in front of a Person of Color. Others may simply not like associating with anyone who is not White.

Sometimes People of Color don't want to be around White-bodied people because they feel like they put up with snubbing from their White co-workers during the workday, and they feel like that is enough. The constant microaggressions are exhausting, and they just can't force themselves to put up with it during their free time. But these social gatherings can be essential to promotions, mentoring, and openings that are not always advertised to the general public. More often than not, managers hire people who went to similar schools as they did, make similar life choices, and are roughly the same age. These are the same people who get invited to the after-work events, get wind of the new openings, are introduced to the manager who has the opening, and are more likely to be recommended for the job. The same social norms are found in schools, from one's circle of influence. People follow the social norm of their peers, family, community, and village, often without much thought to the consequences to themselves and others. We don't see the connection between our actions and our communities, work environments, and families. Our children often socialize the same way we do. Segregation can lead to isolation, social anxiety, and depression.

Forced segregation is a form of oppression and a curtailing of freedom for people on all sides. America was under forced segregation until the 1950s. Segregation not only dictated whom you could have as a neighbor, but whom you could marry. While some may say the White people had the better side of segregation, it is worth considering in order to live in segregation, they also had to give up a part of their freedom and create a myth to justify their perceived freedom. This freedom required they go along with perpetrating violence and abuse on other humans to get along with the rest of the crowd. But living an illusion has a cost.

While financially prosperous, the US ranks third in the world with the most depressed people, according to the World

Health Organization (WHO). Americans have access to every-thing yet suffer high rates of clinical depression. As a nation, we sell high numbers of antidepressants, over-the-counter and prescribed. According to the Centers for Disease Control and Prevention (the CDC), *"Antidepressants have become the most commonly prescribed drugs in the United States. They're prescribed more than drugs to treat high blood pressure, high cholesterol, asthma, or headaches."*

Emotional depression becomes physical pain. Pain med-ication can cause addiction, fueling emotional distress and depression. One might ask, why are we in so much pain?

OUR CIRCLE OF INFLUENCE

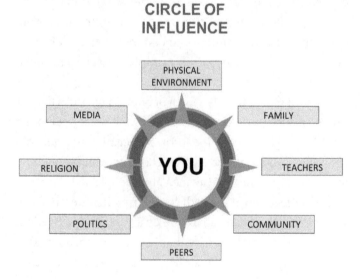

Our circle of influence is made up of the people we have access to and those who have access to us. It is how we learned about racism and segregation even when parents were not being intentional. The circle of influence is made up of our family, community, media, religion, school, peers, and physical environment. As children, we absorb the verbal and non-verbal cues, and we act accordingly.

Segregation was one of the first things established in our nation. During times of slavery, where people lived was determined by their social status. While the slave owners and their families lived in "the big house," the enslaved were relegated to one-room quarters, often housing whole or several families.

In 1896, the Supreme Court ruled in Plessy v. Ferguson that racial segregation in private businesses was constitutional as long as Blacks and Whites were granted equal public accommodations. The problem was separate was never equal. Take schooling, for instance—tax dollars fund schools. Because White people get paid more than People of Color and their houses are priced higher, schools in White neighborhoods have always been better funded than schools in Black and Hispanic communities.

And then there's health. The pandemic of 2020 highlighted the racial disparities not just in health care, but also in education. Because of COVID-19, students had to homeschool, and many Black, Hispanic, and poor White students didn't have access to the technology needed to study at home. As students start falling behind, they will be blamed for not keeping up with their lessons when in reality, their parents did not make enough to afford internet access. In the assumption of separate-but-equal, separate was a reality, equal was not.

HOW RACISM HURTS WHITE PEOPLE

The entitlement founded on supremacy White people experience by having the odds fixed in their favor creates a psycho-emotional gap that disconnects them from themselves and others. As a result, White people often live between entitlement and imposter syndrome, seeking something to fill the void. To survive emotionally in a world created for them, one in which their fundamental free will has been usurped, they collude with the myth of their history. As a result, the mere mention of the words "race" or "racism" triggers their stress response—fight, flight, or paralysis—causing much-needed conversations about race to quickly end.

White people live on a steady diet of racial misinformation sustained by stereotypes, myths, and lies. Our racial conditioning is formed by the information that comes from our circle of influence. For the most part, our circle of influence has lived in segregation, especially if you are a White person.

Your circle of influence shared the secondhand information they had about race. Segregation meant anyone different from you didn't form part of you or your family's circle. Most of the information White people have about People of Color doesn't come from personal experience. The circle of influence has done a pretty good job of keeping White people misinformed about race, and those who are misinformed are bound to miscreate.

On the other hand, White people have been very willing to believe the stories and myths, questioning little and continuing to spread what they were told generation after generation. Myths and lies do not lead to healing. In fact, they add to the dysfunction making it harder for people to heal.

Those who are healthy enough to see the problem blame other White people for their ignorance. They get angry with them for what they don't know and make it challenging to have much-needed conversations on race with other White people.

I challenge you to think about racism as a condition brought about through hundreds of years of conditioning, misinformation, and lies. But it is just that, a condition, one from which those who are willing can heal. From the perspective of racism as a condition, we can see people are suffering, even when they are not aware of it. Their affliction renders them blind to their condition. Therefore, we stop judging their character and look for the cause. Once we understand the cause, we can create a treatment plan for the whole society.

QUESTIONS TO CONSIDER:

- Does thinking about racism as a condition based on historical conditioning make sense to you?

- Do you see racism as something that hurts only People of Color, or does it hurt the whole society?

- Do you believe individual and collective healing is needed?

- How would you go about healing the world from racism?

CHAPTER 3

WHAT IS HEALING AND WHY DO WE NEED IT?

―――

"How do you know you're healing? Because you can finally see the disease."

—MILAGROS PHILLIPS

Emotional pain led me to seek healing. Beyond counseling as my traditional method of healing, I read everything related to personal growth and nontraditional healing I could get my hands on. As I learned, the clouds began to clear, and at some point, I became healthy enough to realize I needed healing. But where to turn? Who could help me? What is healing, and how does healing relate to our wholeness? Why do we even need healing from racism?

When it comes to race and racism, healing is tending to the condition caused by five hundred years of racial conditioning. But inroads are being made. As cities and counties declare racism a public health crisis, perhaps, we can also begin to look at racism as a condition. From that vantage point, we can create a national racial healing campaign and begin to heal the masses.

The nation—indeed, the world—is beginning to look at racism as a social ill affecting the population, according to *USA Today, "the American Public Health Association, which tracks declarations of racism as a public health crisis, lists one hundred forty-five cities and counties across twenty-seven states—up from only seven in 2019. Five were statewide declarations and three were issued by states' governors (Michigan, Wisconsin, and Nevada)."* And the list keeps growing. The death of George Floyd, an African-American man killed by White policeman Derek Chauvin in Minneapolis, Minnesota, on May 25, 2020, as mentioned earlier in this book, has changed the way we look at race.

The incident recorded by bystanders, who were telling Officer Chauvin and the other officers who were kneeling on Mr. Floyd "he can't breathe," quickly went viral over the internet. The video was traumatizing to all who watched and sparked a conscious need for healing. It seemed as if the whole world was traumatized into awakening to what Black people and People of Color have been telling the world for hundreds of years. "Take your knee off our necks. Can't you see? *We can't breathe!"*

My years of experience had taught me people needed intervention. I quickly put together a program to help the community understand racial trauma and manage racial stress offered on the internet and open to the community as mentioned in the introduction. I realized the racial wound had been opened for people who were not used to experiencing racial violence so directly.

I created a program called Race, Trauma, & Healing to help the community understand, deal with emotions, and begin to consider community healing was necessary. So, what is racial healing?

A condition is *"the circumstances affecting the way in which people live or work, especially with regard to their safety or wellbeing."* Conditioning is *"the process of training or accustoming a person or animal to behave in a certain way or to accept certain circumstances"* (*Oxford Online Dictionary*).

Racism is a condition that affects the entire human race—the whole human family. Everywhere "Western civilization" has touched, it has left the violent scar of racism. So, who needs healing? The human family. If we were to look at the condition of racism through the lens of addiction, we might start treating it differently. While addictions, such as alcoholism, are now regarded as medical conditions, racism is a social ill affecting millions worldwide.

Where there's racism, there is psychological and physical violence and abuse, at times leading to death, as we see in the cases of many African-Americans and People of Color all over the world. As happens in families dealing with an alcoholic, one member of the family with an addiction affects the entire family. Therefore, the whole family needs to be treated. In other words, we—members of the human family—all need healing from racism. So, what is healing?

Healing is moving from what is wrong/unhealthy/out of order/dysfunctional/not working correctly or at all and treating it back to wholeness. Healing is the pathway that leads to the cure.

Healing is about seeing, feeling, and awakening to what is not functioning right (dysfunction/malfunction) and is therefore causing pain (physical, mental, emotional, or spiritual).

As a result, what is malfunctioning is wreaking havoc in the body, family, community, country, or world.

Healing is moving toward what is right/functioning/ relieves the pain/leads to health and reminding us of our wholeness. By understanding and connecting the history to the current pain, we can find a cure that stops the pain, causes understanding, and brings about inner and outer peace. Healing is about releasing the racialized, segregated self and joining the human family.

Healing racism is the missing link to our interpersonal and national discourse. Healing, in this case, is about connecting the heart and mind in one coherent whole that allows the body to feel.

Healing is about staying connected to the bodily sensations and discomforts, while peeling away the layers of our racial conditioning. Healing exposes us to uncomfortable truths and holds us compassionately accountable. Rather than being about shaming and blaming, healing racism acknowledges people don't know what they don't know, and learning is essential to the process.

Healing racism is about race literacy. It acknowledges we have all been misinformed when it comes to race, and those who are misinformed are bound to miscreate. Racism was founded on greed and is perpetuated by ignorance. History books and media with partial truths, stereotypes, and violence do not lead to cultural enlightenment.

Healing racism gives context to our discomfort, fragility, and implicit biases. It takes people to the beginning of the problem and connects the past to the present. Healing racism takes people through the stages of healing, which lead to awareness, connection, and action.

Healing racism gives information that leads to transformation. It creates safety for vulnerability, a vital part of healing. Healing allows for tears and emotions, which must be expressed for healing to occur. It cracks us open but doesn't leave us there. Healing takes us to a new awareness of self and treats the whole being—mind, body, spirit, and emotions.

WHAT EXACTLY ARE WE HEALING?

Racism is a problem *for* People of Color, not a problem *of* People of Color. Racism is White people's problem. Blacks and People of Color have to heal the patterns and behaviors they acquired to survive in a White-governed society and in places in the world where White people are the majority. Let's take one group at a time.

White racist attitudes result from years of conditioning through the myth of race, a myth fomented by bad science and the belief in a superior race, as well as the Catholic church and the papal bull known as the Doctrine of Discovery, detailed later in this book. It is further maintained by miseducation—through partial truths and missing history. Centuries of anti-Black and Brown propaganda resulted in normalizing violence against People of Color all over the world.

The payoff for White people is privilege (access, opportunity, immunity, innocence, and freedom). White people need to heal from centuries of living in the poisonous well of racial conditioning, which has turned them consciously and unconsciously racist. As a result, they experience the condition known as racism. So what White people need to heal from is the condition of racism caused by hundreds of years of indoctrination in the myth of race.

White people also need to see how the myth of race and the belief in racism and supremacy oppress them.

They are expected to be silent in the face of institutional and systemic violence toward People of Color. They are expected to go along to get along. Their complacency and complicity with the system of racism dehumanizes them and numbs them to the plight of others. In exchange for their silence, they are lavished with access and opportunities not available to Black people and People of Color. The oppression of compliance is hidden behind privilege for White people, so they don't see it. But their body shows the oppression as depression, a pain that is often hidden behind alcohol, legal and illicit drug use, the constant search for something, their addiction to greed, and their struggle with imposter syndrome.

Black and Brown racial conditioning is the result of living under White-ruled cultures with people indoctrinated in the myth of race and suffering from the condition of racism. They need to heal from the survival patterns acquired over centuries of White rule.

People of Color may need to heal from, among many things, their internalized Stockholm syndrome. In a November 2019 article "What is Stockholm Syndrome and How Does It Affect Us?" by Kimberly Holland and medically reviewed by Timothy J. Legg, PhD, CRNP, *"Stockholm syndrome is a psychological response. It occurs when hostages or abuse victims bond with their captors or abusers. This psychological connection develops over the course of the days, weeks, months, or even years of captivity or abuse."*

Stockholm syndrome may have those who suffer from it identifying with their captors. It shows up as a desire to look like them, act like them, and emulate their responses and behaviors. Some People of Color use bleaching cream to lighten their skin. CNN reports:

A recent study found more than half of 1,992 men and women surveyed about product use in India had tried skin whiteners, and close to half (44.6 percent) felt the need to try such products due to media such as TV and advertisements. Globally, the demand for whiteners is climbing, projected to reach 31.2 billion dollars by 2024, up from 17.9 billion dollars in 2017, especially in Asia, the Middle East, and Africa, according to market intelligence firm Global Industry Analysts. Routine skin whitener use ranges from 25 percent in Mali to 77 percent in Nigeria, and it's 40 percent in China, Malaysia, the Philippines, and South Korea, according to the World Health Organization.

Black people and people of the African Diaspora need to heal from the trauma of slavery and colonization. In her book, *Post Traumatic Slave Syndrome: America's Legacy of Enduring Injury and Healing,* Dr. Joy DeGruy describes:

> *PTSS is a theory that explains the etiology of many of the adaptive survival behaviors in African-American communities throughout the United States and the Diaspora. It is a condition that exists as a consequence of multigenerational oppression of Africans and their descendants resulting from centuries of chattel slavery. A form of slavery predicated on the belief African-Americans were inherently/genetically inferior to Whites. This was then followed by institutionalized racism, which continues to perpetuate injury.*

There is much to be healed in Black and Brown communities.

A DIFFERENT LENS

If we look at racism through the lens of disease, we might consider the possibility of racism as a condition that needs healing. Take, for instance, alcoholism. Those afflicted with the disease of alcoholism benefit from Alcoholics Anonymous (AA), and those who live with the diseased person benefit from Al-Anon, which gives support to the family members. The awareness here is both sets of people, those with the problem and those who live with them, need healing.

WHAT IS NEEDED FOR HEALING?

Healing requires an honest appraisal of one's condition and a willingness to change. It requires understanding and constant vigilance to remain racially sober, awake, and aware. More than a change of mind, we need a change of heart. To heal, we need to face our five-hundred-year-old wound, open it, clean it, and finally, perhaps for the first time, allow it to heal!

As you read through these pages, don't dismiss what feels uncomfortable. Instead, breathe through it. Inhale and exhale slowly and continue on. Know it is not what you are reading that is making you uncomfortable. More than likely, it is that what you are reading has triggered something living in you, something you may have been hiding or may not have been aware of. Don't look to do anything with it now. Simply notice and breathe! If tears come up, don't try to choke them back. Allow your tears to flow as you read. You may wish to note what it was you felt and where in your body you felt it. Keep your journal close by. Healing is what clears away the clouds so we can see our wholeness.

QUESTIONS TO CONSIDER:

- How is racism affecting you?

- Did you feel any sensations in your body as you read this chapter?

- If so, where did you feel these sensations?

- What form of racial conditioning needs to be healed in yourself, your family, and your community?

- What do you think needs to happen for racial healing to occur?

- How would you go about it?

CHAPTER 4

THE DIFFERENCE BETWEEN ANTI-RACISM & HEALING RACISM

"Being anti-racist is much needed in today's climate. But to be anti-anything is exhausting. At some point, even the best anti-racist will need to seek healing."

—MILAGROS PHILLIPS

Anti-racism work gives an understanding of the fundamental structure of our racist systems. It wakes people up to the realities of racism and its impact on Black people, Indigenous people, and People of Color, also known as "BIPOC." Anti-racism work is much needed, but it often leaves participants stuck in guilt, shame, and anger. This prevents them from moving forward and doing the vital work needed to change our society. Remember racism is a problem *for* People of Color; it is not the problem *of* People of Color. To solve racism, the whole community needs to be involved. We can't afford to leave anyone behind.

Anti-racism is about what is happening in our outer world. Healing racism is about staying aware of what is happening in the outer world and how it affects our inner world. Healing requires we pay attention to mind, body, spirit, and emotions and learn to manage our actions, reactions, and interactions. In healing, we do all of this while staying connected to what's happening in the world around us. Healing racism is about remaining whole in spite of it.

Healing racism is the missing link to our current discourse on race. It uses fundamental history, science, and storytelling to weave a tapestry that connects the past to the present. Healing racism takes people through the stages of healing, which leads to awareness, connection, and action.

Healing racism gives information that leads to transformation. It creates safety for all and allows for tears and emotions, which must be expressed for healing to occur. Healing is about treating the whole being—mind, body, spirit, and emotions.

You will definitely want to be against racism to start healing by doing things like speaking out against it and believing People of Color when they tell you something is wrong. However, healing requires a different set of skills than those we have been operating under and a new, steady diet of fresh and creative ideas. Healing requires we hold space for emotions such as anger, frustration, and pain. It requires patience. People didn't get this way overnight, so healing will take time. It means knowing people are going to get it wrong, mistakes will be made, and, at times, we may regress. In healing racism, we know we all have triggers, and we may well not know what may trigger a person.

Healing work means dealing with messy emotions, and it prompts individuals to delve into those emotions rather than suppress them. It welcomes tears; it asks where in your body you are feeling those tears and what memories and family information those tears bring up for you. It requires a keen awareness of self and others and compassion for both. It requires an understanding of history to connect the past with the present. Healing is understanding how historical traumas impact us across generations.

Leaving behind the racially conditioned self requires humility, self-responsibility, and a commitment to change. Healing invites us to go through the shadow and own our share of it. Rather than see the problem as out-there, it leads us to see how we unconsciously collude with the problem. Healing requires a willingness to acknowledge the pain and do something about it. Healing involves seeing the emotional distress as a warning something needs to be done or the problem will continue and even worsen. Healing is about understanding the conditions that have led to our racial conditioning and the events, circumstances, and methods used to get us to adhere to that conditioning.

Healing gives us a foundation for our actions, reactions, and interactions. It lets us take responsibility for making the changes needed to leave behind the racialized self and embrace the oneness of the human family. It allows us to see how our unwillingness to face our shadow and its subsequent silence affects the world around us. Healing gives us techniques to calm the spirit and stay sane in a toxic environment.

Healing is worth the discomfort! On the other side of healing is our personal and collective liberation. Because healing racism is about healing our relationship to ourselves and others, those who embark on the journey find they heal other areas of their lives as well.

Here are some things you will need to begin your journey of healing.

Humility – When we think we already know it all, we stop learning. Be curious and acknowledge you don't know what you don't know.

Emotional Healing – Racism is personal. Eventually, someone has or will say something that triggers you. You may feel hurt, angry, or even enraged. Don't hide from the pain.

Physical Healing – Whether you are aware of it or not, racism lives in your body. In my seminars, participants are shown how to find where racism lives in their body and what to do about it. To find where racism lives in your body, do this simple exercise. Take a deep breath and blow it out. Close your eyes. Get quiet and focus on your body. Bring your awareness to the inside of your body and say to yourself, silently and gently, three times the word "racism." Then take a deep breath and say to yourself the word "peace" three times. Notice the difference in the way your body feels with each of those words.

Mental Healing – We have been told many stories about race and racism, most of them untrue. The bad news is we are excellent learners. The good news is we are *excellent learners*. We can replace what we've learned with new and different information. Transforming five hundred years of conditioning is not a mental/cognitive or academic exercise. If it were, we would have solved racism a long time ago.

Spiritual Healing – Racism is America's spiritual dilemma. It has been since the days when people would brutalize enslaved persons, work them, and sometimes beat them to death. They would go to church on Sunday to profess religious values of love and justice and brutalize their slaves again on Monday.

America likes to see itself as a beacon of light in the world. We're the good guys. Racism doesn't fit into the narrative of "the free and the brave." We avoid stories that make us look like weak bullies. If you visit the bully's house, you walk away feeling sorry for them. You find the father abuses the bully, the mother drinks to escape her plight, and the grandparents still humiliate and infantilize the bully's father, in front of his children. Meanwhile, the bully brags about his great home life and swears he doesn't need healing. In the meantime, the bully thinks he needs another kid to bully or a war to fight to feel better about himself.

The truth is without consciously seeking healing, we don't stand much of a chance. You see, even "good guys" are racist when they are raised in a racist system with racist institutions by parents who themselves internalized racism. At that level, one can't help but act racism out in interpersonal relationships since everything in our environment has normalized the dysfunction.

Healing, however, helps us establish new norms and see new possibilities. It relieves guilt and shame and keeps us growing throughout our lives.

QUESTIONS TO CONSIDER:

- Have you attended anti-racism seminars?

- Have you participated in healing racism work?

- How did it make you feel?

- Do you see a need for healing?

CHAPTER 5

RACE, LATITUDE, & ATTITUDE

———

"Our goal should be to understand our differences."
—JAMES D. WATSON

In the realm of the living, life holds the highest value since, without it, we cease to exist on the planet. Some things are essential to our physical survival and life on Earth. Remember learning about Maslow's hierarchy of needs in school? At the bottom of the triangle was survival (clothing, food, and shelter). If we value life, then we also value what sustains it. But the value we place on what sustains us—objects, relationships, places, and even time—is predicated on where in the world our ancestors lived, developed, and thrived.

Food, clothing, shelter, and natural resources are predicated on where your country is placed on the global axis.

In 2006, while recording an episode of *Spirit in Action*, a radio show I once co-hosted, I interviewed an industrial psychologist named Dr. Edwin Nichols. Dr. Nichols helped develop what was once called a theory, now known as the philosophy of axiology. Axiology is the study of values based on culture and environment. What axiology teaches is people developed values based on where they lived in the world and what helped them survive, namely clothing, food, and shelter. In other words, your latitude may be governing your attitude.

The best way to explain axiology is to break down the components of the patterns. As you read, keep in mind these are ancient survival patterns, and we see modern-day attitudes that reflect these patterns. As you go through the story, notice if you get any sensations in your body. First, here are some things you will need to understand the story.

Wherever you live in the world, food is necessary to your survival. If your biological tribe developed in a cold climate, they had about three months out of the year to grow food. Nine months out of the year, except for the evergreens, the trees and plants are bare.

Food, being the object of the highest value, becomes focal to the community. To have food, one had to pay attention and keep track of the following:

Time – Miss the growing season and you will not survive. The efficiency of time is essential; shortcuts are needed as not to miss the growing season.

Preservation – Keep the grain until you can grow and harvest more the subsequent season.

Ways of knowing – Count, measure, repeat. Allocate the amount to make the grain last until the next growing season.

Clothing – Keep the body warm during the cold winters.

Shelter – Strong enough to protect you and the grain.

Guards – The food had to be protected from other villages and from those who would take more than their share.

Relationships – They are transactional, quid-pro-quo arrangements.

The list above represents ways of seeing the world, ways of knowing, and ways of staying alive. These patterns of behavior work well in a cold environment. But what happens when someone from a cold climate visits a warm environment? To understand that we have to know what they value based on their proximity to the equator and the intensely hot sun.

If your tribe developed in warmer climates, here are some things they did and did not value. Preservation of wealth (the object) is central to society. The one who controls the grain is sure to survive.

Time – Where food grows 365 days a year, time is not of the essence. In warm climates, there's always something growing. Food is freely supplied by nature. Your view of the world is that of abundance. If the papaya is not in season, the mango is, or the avocado, or the banana. Food is plentiful and readily available at all times. They have a different relationship with time.

Preservation – You don't preserve food because the heat makes it rot. Besides, there will be more available tomorrow, so you don't worry about survival.

Ways of knowing were more intuitive, grounded on their relationship to the soil, sky, and nature.

Clothing – Not necessary. It's hot.

Shelter – Simple materials found in their surroundings. Anyone can build shelter, even a child or a pregnant woman. Shelter was more about protection from the heat and the sun.

Guard – Animals can kill you in the night while you sleep.

Relationships – These people placed their highest value in relationships because there was more time to socialize. You don't want to take what is not yours because it would "bring shame" upon yourself and your family.

Consider this: when people are in survival fear, the primordial brain takes over. Here's a story I use in my seminars to illustrate axiology.

LATITUDE, FOOD, & WAR

Let's say the crops in your village (Village A) didn't do well this year, and the grain produced will not allow you and your villagers to survive the winter. You're looking for solutions to your problem, and you find out Village B, a few miles away, grew a bumper crop. You make a journey with some men to negotiate for some of their grain, but they refuse. You go home and tell your community Village B refused to negotiate and they will not share the food. You know if you don't get the grain, many will die this winter. Your own life is in peril. So, you offer to get the grain from Village B. But to do so, you will need the firstborn male from every family and five percent of the grain from each of the villagers when you return. The villagers agree. Remember, this is for survival.

You go to the next village, in the middle of the night, while most are sleeping, kill the men and the elderly, rape the women and children, and enslave anyone who survives. You now have wealth, an army, and a free labor force. You deem yourself the ruler of the people, or they may have you as their ruler. After all, you just saved the village from starvation, and your plan worked brilliantly. The highest value is in the object that helped you survive—food.

As the ruler, you get to make the laws, and if the villagers disagree, you get your army to imprison them, throw them in the donjon, feed them to the lions, or kill them. You make sure your army protects you from the villagers. You live with a constant fear the villagers will revolt against you, so you need constant protection. The problem is the atrocities committed have not only traumatized you and those you took to war, but that trauma will be passed on to your progeny for generations to come. And the same will be true for all those who survived.

The way to keep the villagers on your side is to go to another village and take what they have to ensure their continued survival. The people in Village A find the way they are getting their grain repugnant, but this is about survival. Don't complain. You're living better than you were before. And you're working less because the enslaved took your place in the field. The people in Village A agree to support the new method of getting their needs met. So, you do this over and over again until it becomes the "new normal." The villagers give up their sons and part of their wealth in exchange for safety and food. The collective agreement is a collusion of silence—partly because you don't want to rock the boat, and partly because you are afraid of the ruler and your peers.

By the time the next generation comes of age, heroic stories have been developed and past wars romanticized. The new generation can't wait to come of age and join the group of men who conquer, steal, and enslave, for they are the heroes of their village, they are the celebrated ones. And while some still find their ways grotesque, not to mention the lives lost, they continue to go along with what has become the new normal because protesting could mean their lives. Don't make waves; you now have clothes, food, and shelter in abundance. How you got it haunts you. You live with the fear strangers can't be trusted because they could mean you harm. There is plenty of food to preserve. There are woven fabrics, rugs, and furs to keep you warm. But inside, you live with the fear this could end and what you have may still not be enough.

Seeing the success of their ways, the leaders now venture into other lands, lands that are very far away from the village a few miles down the road. There is now a template. All you have to do is repeat it.

LATITUDE AND IMPOSED ATTITUDE

Axiology works well in its own environment. The problem starts when one group tries to impose their axiology on a different environment with people who have different values. We falter when we impose survival patterns on people, and places where they don't belong because of their placement on the global axis. We live in a world where cold climate people have imposed their ways on warm climate people for hundreds of years.

Why is this important to understanding racism? Our values dictate our actions, reactions, and interactions. They also govern our expectations and our beliefs. In a world of scarcity, people become objectified, and relationships become transactional. People's value is in what they can contribute and not their intrinsic human value. Humans are objects to be colonized, used, and consumed, and so are places on the Earth and even in space.

LATITUDE AND RECEPTIVE ATTITUDE

I come from one of those warm climate countries. I still remember my first gift-giving with an American child. I spoke very little English at the time, and my friend did not speak Spanish. I had fun with my friend; even though we spoke different languages, we always laughed.

One day, I was shopping with my mother, and I asked her if I could buy a gift for my friend. She said yes, and I picked out a decorative pin for her hair. It was not a special occasion, but in my culture, one does not need a special occasion to celebrate people and life. Before she even opened the gift, she was apologizing for not having a present for me.

It had never occurred to me to give her a gift so I could get something in return. In my family, I learned a gift was something you give and let go of, no strings attached. Gifts are not transactional. That's what business is for. To me, it just seemed so strange she would think I should warn her about the gift so she could have one for me. To her, receiving a gift without something to give in exchange was not natural. It's not one is good, and one is bad, one is right, and one is wrong; it's just different. To me, transactional giving took all the fun out of gifting. For me, that just wasn't natural.

LATITUDE AND THE ATTITUDE OF ENTITLEMENT

Here is a more poignant example of how latitude governs attitude. Let's travel to the 1400s in Europe. You have lived in a cold climate all your life, and you travel to the Caribbean. Natives are living on the island where you just landed. Your first impression is they are savages because they are not wearing any clothes. Their idea of shelter is a hut made of sticks and leaves. Their ways of worshiping are strange to you because they worship nature, and they gave you food without an expectation of getting anything in return. Strange people indeed!

From a different perspective, seeing you perspire in your wool and many layers of clothing causes natives to laugh. They quickly realize they have to hide their women and girls, as seeing them fully undressed causes you arousal (you're not used to that). They are adorned in raw gold and stones, whose value you appraise as you try to communicate in your language, which they do not understand.

You think they are unwell because they play with the gold and the silver, like children with marbles. They seem to hold no value for the precious metals and stone, and as far as you can see, they don't know what to do with it. What they play with, like children, could make you rich back in the old country. So, you decide to kill them all and take their possessions to a place that can really appreciate their value. You have a history of killing others for their property. It was one of the ways you survived. But the trauma of that history now lives in your blood. You have a system that has worked for you in the past, and it will work again and again. And every time you went to war for property that was not yours, you compromised yourself, those you took with you, and those you left back home for generations to come. You thought you were just compromising the recipients of the violence.

Many myths have been created to excuse violent behaviors and the mistreatment of People of Color. This attitude of entitlement, and the objectification of human life, led to the Doctrine of Discovery, a papal decree that colonized the world, enslaved millions, and took the Indigenous people's land. This doctrine still governs us today. You'll learn more about the doctrine in the chapter on history.

Why is all of this important? Europe colonized and enslaved most of the countries along the equator. That was not a coincidence. Those formerly colonized countries make up the bulk of what is known as "third world" countries, known more recently as developing countries. And while these countries are rich in food and natural resources, their people live below the poverty line. Most of the inhabitants in these countries are Black and People of Color. If we are going to heal, we need the context of our history to understand the way things are.

LATITUDE, ATTITUDE, AND THE MYTH OF THE ANGRY BLACK WOMAN

I am a Black woman. My mother and sister were Black women. My daughter is a Black woman. My aunts were Black women. I have Black nieces, great-nieces, and great-great-nieces. I have Black women colleagues, friends from North, Central, and South America, Africa, the Middle East, and Europe, and none of them would classify as angry. That doesn't mean we don't get angry. We are human. But none of these women walk around angry. I have, at one time or another, met women of all shades who had a chip on their shoulder, but that is rare. At any rate, who could blame us? Women have been used and abused throughout the history of humanity in ways which one can't help but admire our resilience. Anger is not relegated to one race of people. So, where did this idea of the "angry Black woman" come from?

Let's go back to Europe and consider who could build a shelter. If a woman was kicked out of her home in the middle of the winter with no resources, she knew death was imminent. When men got tired of their wives or had a new preference, they would put them out. If they had enough rank, they would accuse the women of some crime and have them imprisoned, beheaded, or burned at the stake. The later historical versions of this treatment of women were to put them in a mental institution. This became such a popular practice that laws were instituted that basically said if a man commits his wife to a mental institution, he could not marry while she was still alive. Now, if you knew that if you didn't behave, this would be your destiny, you might be more likely to be compliant, quiet, and complacent. The fate of women who fought came down to the stories of women like Joan of Arc, who led the French army victoriously against the English in 1429 during the Hundred Year War, and Princess Sela of Norway, who fought valiantly against King Horwendil, only to be killed by him c. 420 CE. These women were warriors, but what of the average woman? Her fate was entwined with those who could keep her safe.

Now, let's travel south to women in Africa, along the equatorial band. Prior to colonization, African society was more egalitarian. Often, women fought alongside the men in resistance to colonization. Their ability to build shelter, and the abundance of food, meant even if they were thrown out of the hut, they could survive. This meant women were less dependent on men for their survival. They were more likely to speak their minds. They led armies of women as well as armies of men. Women like Kahina, a Berber woman who fought bravely against Ramesses II, pharaoh of the Nineteenth Dynasty of Egypt, and the Arabs in 702 CE. Queen Candace of Ethiopia, c. 330 BCE, who battled Alexander the Great while on top of a war elephant. She also faced many great militaries. Even after losing an eye, she fought fiercely against Rome. There were countless women warriors, but the average woman was a lot less dependent on men for their survival because of the availability of shelter and food. So, women would be more assertive and not face the same dangers as women in cold climates.

With colonization, women were reduced to property and servitude all over the colonialized world. Men of their own culture began to treat the women as did their colonizers. Women lost their place in society. The same conditioning that leads to seeing Black people as bad, wrong, violent, and ugly has followed Black women and Women of Color for centuries. Black men are also seen as angry and feared for White people's internalized misperceptions. They even lose their lives over the myth of Black anger, a myth that leads even trained safety officers to see weapons in the hands of Black people even when there are none.

QUESTIONS TO CONSIDER:

- Did you learn about axiology in school?

- How does the philosophy of axiology feel in your body?

- Does axiology seem plausible to you?

- If you've traveled to different parts of the world, have you noticed people value time differently?

- Do you come from a culture that embraces change?

- Does the cultural group you identify with value preserving—antiques, the status quo, food in cans and bottles?

- How could understanding attitudes based on latitude help us be more patient and compassionate with one another?

- How are women valued in your culture?

CHAPTER 6

THE ROLE OF EMOTIONS

———

"Your intellect may be confused, but your emotions will never lie to you."

—ROGER EBERT

Emotions are essential to the healing of racism. Healing requires vulnerability, sensitivity, and compassion. When it comes to emotions, humans are either neutral, in love, or fearful. When our needs are met, we tend to be in a positive flow of emotions. When our needs are not met, our emotions are the opposite. Let's break this down and as we do, think of how racism affects you. For the sake of this book, we will look at the emotions of love and fear, as it is rare people are neutral about race and racism.

The emotion of fear has many feelings associated with it. When we are in fear, we may feel anger, rage, sadness, frustration, disappointment, distrust, anxiety, disconnection, and much more.

Under the emotion of love, we experience feelings of connection, fulfillment, safety, security, and trust. In love, we feel understood, accepted, empowered, inspired, and cared for. The emotion of love allows us to experience joy, happiness, and freedom. Below is a short list of feelings listed under the corresponding emotion.

EMOTIONS LIST

Emotion LOVE	Emotion FEAR
FEELINGS	**FEELINGS**
ACCEPTANCE	ANGER
SAFE	DISCONTENT
HAPPY	ANXIOUS
JOY	STRESS
UNDERSTAND	IMPATIENCE
SUPPORTED	TRIGGERED
SECURE	TIRED
APPRECIATED	HURT
CONNECTED	OFFENDED
EMPOWERED	UNSAFE
HEARD	INSECURE
FREEDOM	INADEQUATE
SEEN	DREAD
CONFIDENT	WORRY

Babies—and we were all babies at one point—are born with only two fears—falling and loud noises—according to Nadia Kounang's article "What Is the Science behind Fear?" "*A 1960 study evaluated depth perception among six- to fourteen-month-old infants, as well as young animals. Researchers placed the subjects on a platform that had plexiglass just beyond its edge to see how many of the subjects would actually step over the 'visual cliff.' Most of the subjects—both children and animals—didn't go 'over' and step out onto the plexiglass. The fear of falling is an instinct necessary for the survival of many species"* (CNN Health, October 29, 2015).

In the same article, *"When you hear loud sounds, you most likely will react with a fight or flight type response. It's called your 'acoustic startle reflex,'"* said Seth Norrholm, a translational neuroscientist at Emory University. Norrholm explained if a sound is loud enough, *"you're going to duck down your head. Loud noises typically mean startling. That circuitry is innate. It's a response we have that signals something dangerous may be around the corner."*

Two fears, that's all we bring to the planet. We learned everything else you see on the previous list. The bad news is we learned those fears from our circle of influence. The good news is also we learned it because everything we learn can be unlearned and replaced with something new.

Racial conditioning has been based on violence and is maintained through violence. When it comes to the two emotions, violence is a form of fear. We know violence begets violence. In other words, violence keeps us stuck in a cycle of its own making. To stop the violence, we need to think differently and consider the power contained in the emotion of love. But how do you do that when there's continuous violence coming at you? How do you stay centered in a world where you are constantly violated?

To heal, we need to cross the bridge that takes us away from fear and lands us squarely on the road to love. But before that happens, healing moves us back and forth to get us unstuck. Healing helps us to see, feel, and experience the difference between fear and love and gives us the opportunity to enact our power of choice. Healing asks us where we will visit and where we will live. We will live in love or in fear.

What emotion will we call home? To answer this question, consider humanity's true nature.

If you ask the average person, out of the two emotions, what is our true nature, many people will say fear. But if babies are only born with two fears and everything else is learned, is our true nature really fear? Let's take it a bit further and consider what emotion makes us feel safe and comfortable. Are you comfortable when you feel angry, disconnected, unsafe, insecure, and closed off? Are you comfortable when you feel accepted, cared for, relaxed, joyous, peaceful, and at ease? The very reason we want to heal from racism is we are so uncomfortable with it we can't even have a conversation about it.

The bridge from fear to love is compassion and forgiveness. Forgiveness is one people really struggle with when it comes to the issue of race. Hundreds of years of violence, theft, imprisonment, and continued daily aggressions—how can one ever forgive that? Yet forgiveness is part of the healing process as you will see later in this book. And it is one of the ways we end the cycle of violence.

QUESTIONS TO CONSIDER:

- When it comes to racism, where do your emotions run?

- When it comes to race, do you often find yourself getting angry with others?

- How does anger feel in your body?

- How can your emotions serve you?

- Is there someone in your life who you can speak with about your emotions in dealing with racism?

CHAPTER 7

TRAUMA

———

"Trauma is a fact of life. It does not,
however, have to be a life sentence."

—PETER A. LEVINE

I am not a trauma therapist. I learned about trauma as a way of caring for myself because I do race work, and race work is toxic. People send me all kinds of horrific things, like videos of hangings and a policeman who picked up a woman and body-slammed her, so she hit her head against the wall and cracked her skull. They send me information about riots not found in school history books. Not meaning to cause me harm, they are merely sharing news and information. So, I had to learn self-care.

I've taken some trauma courses with the National Institute for the Clinical Application of Behavioral Medicine. They do excellent work with trauma. I've also taken courses on cultural somatics because racial trauma lives in the body, whether you are a White person, a Person of Color, or a Black person. I've also taken the racialized trauma course with Resmaa Menakem, the author of *My Grandmother's Hands*. I have spent countless hours researching the effects of trauma on the body, emotions, and the mind. I did this research not to teach but because I needed to heal. In this chapter, I share information to give you a basic understanding of racial trauma and its effect on all our lives, especially the lives of the Black, Indigenous, and People of Color.

UNDERSTANDING TRAUMA

First, let's define trauma. According to the Merriam-Webster online dictionary, trauma is an injury, such as a wound, to living tissue. It is also a disordered psychic and behavioral state resulting from severe mental or emotional stress or physical injury, or an emotional upset.

There have been changes in the definition of trauma. Trauma was first used to describe the shock experienced by survivors of horrific events. You had to be a soldier or survivor of war to be seen as traumatized. But now, there's a broader definition of trauma. Trauma can be psychological, emotional, or physical injury. Repeated racial stress causes emotional injury. Experiences such as living with housing insecurity, living in an unsafe neighborhood, receiving threats to your life, or experiencing highly stressful events that occur repeatedly qualify as traumatic events.

Trauma can be primary, which means you are the subject of the injury. Or it can be secondary; you could witness, hear about, or read about a traumatic event.

In May of 2020, many of us saw the three policemen kneeling on George Floyd, two on his body to hold him down and one directly on his neck until the breath went out of his body. Some see these kinds of events repeatedly throughout their lives. People who have these intense experiences are traumatized and retraumatized. What we know today about trauma is traumatized people traumatize others, and that trauma gets passed on through epigenetics. Epigenetics is the study of how your experiences, environment, and behavior affect the way your genes work.

Dr. Rachel Yehuda is a professor of psychiatry and neuroscience, the Vice Chair for Veterans Affairs in the Psychiatry Department, and the Director of the Traumatic Stress Studies Division at Mount Sinai School of Medicine. Dr. Yehuda explains:

We already know this (stress-related) gene is a gene that contributes to risk for depression and post-traumatic stress disorder. When we looked at children of patients suffering from PTSD, their children also had an epigenetic change in the same spot on the stress-related gene. Dr. Joy DeGruy, author of *Post Traumatic Slave Syndrome,* said, *We're talking about multiple, race-related traumas for hundreds of years. Not only are you traumatized indirectly, you see your friends, your cousins, and everyone in your environment being sold away, beaten, mutilated, raped, and eventually lynched. Is it possible those people were able to escape stress-related illness? No* (The Atlantic Star Video, *Scientists Are Now Saying the Trauma of Slavery May Be Encoded,* May 27, 2016). Much of what we now know about trauma and epigenetics came from studying survivors of the Holocaust, and soldiers returning from war.

When we speak about racial trauma, what we are talking about is life-course-stress, continuous violence, both physical and mental, and repeated daily slights that add up. In other words, accumulated stressors over time and an undercurrent of not feeling safe in the world. One of the ways racial conditioning lives in People of Color today is through decontextualized historical trauma.

Something you don't know may have happened to your ancestors. Your ancestors may have been violated, or they may have been the violators. We have this belief that those who perpetrate violent acts are somehow exempt from that violence they impose on others and its aftermath. Nothing could be further from the truth. While the violence may look different on the perpetrator's side, we now know through the study of trauma and epigenetics their progeny has not been spared the trauma their predecessors imposed on others. The children of the perpetrators of violence can also be subject to their parents' trauma. And without the benefit of the context, this trauma can be expressed in implicit and explicit ways.

This implicit trauma is held in the body, and people act, react, and interact out of that trauma. How White people carry the trauma of racism, and act out of it, is by maintaining a culture of silence, fear of speaking out about racial injustices, and continually perpetrating or allowing repeated violence against People of Color. White people carry an unconscious fear of revolt and attack that gets triggered by Black and Brown bodies. They have been conditioned to believe Black and Brown bodies are to be feared. They don't realize what they really fear is that they might be the recipients of the violence they and their ancestors have perpetrated for centuries. Then there is also an undercurrent of restlessness that could be getting triggered by living on land taken through violence. The restless spirit is seeking a balance that can only be brought about through justice. Life is a continuum. Nothing is random.

People don't know what they may be carrying in their bodies because they're not connecting what they're feeling and experiencing at the moment to something that happened many generations ago. One of the ways to know is if you're having an irrational reaction to a person, word, event, or even a look someone gives you. Notice if your reaction is normal for the situation, or are you overreacting?

This segment is directed at White-bodied people. When it comes to your fear of Black people—particularly fear of Black men—ask yourself: Is your level of fear natural? If this were a White person, would you have the same reaction? Do you have a natural fear of People of Color because you have had a personal, negative experience, or have you been conditioned and trained to fear People of Color in general? Do you fear all White men because of Jeffrey Dahmer? He was known as the Milwaukee Cannibal, an American serial killer and sex offender who committed the murder and dismemberment of seventeen men and boys from 1978 to 1991. Do you fear White men because of David Berkowitz, the Boston Strangler, Ted Bundy, John Wayne Gacy? Then why do you fearfully lock your car at the very sight of a Black man? What is it about Black and Brown skin that makes you think danger or harm?

Trauma gets passed on for several generations. An article in the "Health Science" section of the *Washington Post* entitled, "Study Finds that Fear Can Travel Quickly Through Generations of Mice DNA," outlined an experiment that has come to be known as the "cherry blossom experiment." Researchers pumped the fragrance of cherry blossom into cages filled with mice, and every time they did, they would use mild electric shock on the mice. This would cause pain and would traumatize the mice. They found after a while that they didn't have to electrocute the mice. All they had to do was pump the cherry blossom fragrance and the mice would act traumatized. The mice were mated two weeks later, and they found the next generation acted more traumatized than the first generation. I have a personal theory about that, and that is that the first generation of mice knew something was happening to them. The second generation had no context for what they were experiencing when they smelled the oil. All they knew was how what the smell of the oil made them feel, and they acted out of what they were feeling.

> *In the experiment, researchers taught male mice to fear the smell of cherry blossoms by associating the scent with mild foot shocks. Two weeks later, they bred with females. The resulting pups were raised to adulthood having never been exposed to the smell. Yet when the critters caught a whiff of it for the first time, they suddenly became anxious and fearful. They were even born with more cherry-blossom-detecting neurons in their noses and more brain space devoted to cherry-blossom-smelling. The memory transmission extended out another generation when these male mice were bred, and similar results were found. Neuroscientists at Emory University found genetic markers, thought to be wiped clean before birth, were used to transmit a single traumatic experience across generations, leaving behind traces in the behavior and anatomy of future pups (*Washington Post, *December 7, 2013).*

Researchers found the mice acted traumatized up to six generations after the first generation. That's a full seven generations. It seems our knowledge of trauma being passed on for several generations even goes back to ancient books. Here is a sample: *"Visiting the iniquity of the fathers upon the children, and upon the children's children, unto the third and to the fourth generation"* (King James Bible, Exodus 34:7). If you substitute the word "iniquity" for trauma, it seems to me we've known trauma gets passed on for many generations for a long time. So continual institutional and systemic racism adds to People of Color's re-traumatization and post-traumatic stress: daily, micro-, and macroaggressions, negative media images and stereotypes, and the hierarchical caste system. But remember you can't traumatize others without the perpetrator being compromised. So, every time People of Color are traumatized, White people become more frightened, and thereby, more frightening. Now, let's explore this idea based on colorism.

Colorism is making comparisons based on skin color and the discrimination that may come out of those comparisons. The idea is the lighter your skin and the more European one looks, the better one is treated. The darker the skin, the worse one gets treated. You know, the everyday stuff like driving while Black, walking while Black, talking while Black, and much, much more. Skin color has even been linked to Black and Brown people's salaries. The darker one's skin, the lower the salary. Economic violence is something that came with colonization and enslavement, and even that is divided by skin color. In their study, published in January of 2018, "The Effects of Skin Tone, Height, and Gender on Earnings," Devaraj, Quigley, and Patel explain it here:

> *The literature on skin tone bias has been developing for decades in various fields. Sociologists have long considered skin tone bias across the world as a social issue with deeply ingrained historical roots. Hunter, for example, notes skin tone bias was apparent as slave owners "typically used skin tone as a dimension*

of hierarchy on the plantation;" lighter-skinned slaves typically worked in homes while slave owners assigned darker-skinned slaves to work in the fields. In modern society, sociologists have studied the influence of skin tone bias in a number of decisions, from hiring to marriage. Within the field of economics, the topic of skin tone bias has become more visible relatively recently. Several studies have linked skin tone to income levels, with the overall finding being darker skin tone seems to be negatively related to income. Kreisman and Rangel's study nests skin tone within race (i.e., Black and White), allowing the opportunity to (1) control for intergroup gaps in the labor market between Black and White individuals and (2) to assess intra-racial gaps in labor market outcomes among Black individuals of varying skin tone. Among other findings, their results indicate that controlling for background characteristics such as childhood circumstances, education, and skills reduces the income gap between Blacks and Whites in their sample by half but has a much lower effect on reducing the income gap between light and dark among those who identified as Black. Black people and People of Color have to face all of this and more.

As a nation, we are very good at looking at numbers when it comes to racial disparities. We love to research. Indeed, our epistemology is based on counting and measuring. We know the wealth gap numbers. We count how many more Black and Brown people there are in jail compared to White people. We speak of higher counts of high blood pressure, diabetes, and colon cancer in the African-American community. Rarely do we speak of the centuries of trauma perpetrated on Black and Brown people that cause the high numbers of stress-related illnesses. We don't talk about the centuries of violence, forced poverty, theft of land, forced human labor camps, slavery, prisons, and systemic inequality that have affected and continue to affect People of Color. We don't think about how all the aforementioned affects families and communities. We don't think about how unsafe all of this makes People of Color feel. And we don't consider how the trauma caused by all the above is being carried in Black and Brown bodies. We don't look at how generational/historical trauma, repeated traumatization, and microaggressions (brief, daily assaults) and macroaggressions affect the mental, emotional, and thereby physical health of Individuals and Communities of Color. We never discuss how this may be affecting White communities, who endanger the lives of People of Color because they don't feel safe. And when you look to speak with them about racism, their stress response gets triggered.

When we consider the level of continual stress and re-traumatization Black and Brown bodies live under, it's a wonder they are as healthy as they are. The resilience exhibited by People of Color, who live under racial stress and pressure, is really quite extraordinary.

"For every thousand people beating at the branches of evil, there's only one beating at the root."
—HENRY DAVID THOREAU

When it comes to race and racism, we want to solve it at the branches and the leaves. That's very difficult to do. A deep problem requires depth of healing. Trauma is at the very root of the racism problem. To solve racism, we need to be trauma-informed, and you'll see why as we go deeper into the history.

QUESTIONS TO CONSIDER:

- Do you believe racism can be traumatic for People of Color? If so, give examples.

- Do you believe racism is traumatic for White people? If so, give examples.

- Do you see how racism is a social health crisis?

- Do you believe health care providers would benefit their patients by being racial-trauma-informed?

- Should medical schools offer race trauma training?

CHAPTER 8

WHY HISTORY MATTERS

———

"People are trapped in history and history is trapped in them."
—JAMES BALDWIN

Why do we need to become literate about race in America? Who cares about the past? I'm concerned with what is happening right now! Why do we have to talk about things that happened hundreds of years ago?

Why? Because the country is still divided along racial lines. We need to speak about what happened hundreds of years ago because the effects of what happened are still with us today, and the history has not been properly explored. We need to unravel the threads, put in the missing pieces, and connect the dots of our experiences in order to make sense of them. We need to listen to each other and understand there have been two Americas, separate but not necessarily equal. The past does not have to equal the future. We need our history to heal. This is why when you go to the doctor, the first information they gather from you is your family history.

History quickens the healing process by giving us information that puts things in perspective. History connects us to the continuum that is life. History gives context to our current events and connects us to those who came before us. It reminds us of their resilience, which lives in us, and we can tap into for our healing. History helps us understand our current behaviors and allows us to choose differently. It can make us more compassionate as we begin to understand how we do what we do and why we do what we do.

We do our best to protect our progeny, but sometimes, all we do is pass on our fears.

My mother was adamant no daughter of hers would ever work as a domestic, so she made certain her girls had a skill that would allow them to be self-supporting without needing to work in someone's home.

In the Dominican Republic, where I was born and spent the first ten years of my life, in the 1950s and '60s, Black girls were seen as the natural applicants to the post of domestic work, and in my mother's mind, this meant exposure to all sorts of abusive experiences.

Interestingly enough, my mother had high regard for domestic workers and treated all the women who worked in our home with compassion, generosity, and respect, and she demanded that of all of us.

It would never occur to me or any of my siblings to yell at anyone who worked for us, although that did not stop my mother from yelling at us.

I never heard my mother say none of us would ever be domestics, but it was understood.

It was one of those silent expressions that just hangs in the air. It was a family secret, or at least it was linked to one I would discover as an adult. The discovery of that history helped my world make sense.

"If it's hysterical, it's historical."

—RESMAA MENAKEM

The only time I ever saw my mother yell at one of the women who worked for us was when I had asked the woman who did our laundry (by hand) to teach me how to wash. I was seven years old and more interested in playing with the bubbles than washing clothes, but when my mother saw me with my hands in the washtub, she was incensed. I had never seen her so angry with someone who worked for us. I was hauled away and told never to do that. I felt terrible for the woman and was angry with my mother, who had often spoiled my fun. In time, I had forgotten the incident.

One evening, while visiting my only sister, who was nearly three decades my senior, she began to speak about my grandmother. I loved my grandmother, though we rarely spoke. She was eighty-one when I was born, and I still remember running to her for comfort, support, and hiding when I needed it. She spoke up for me and defended me when I got in trouble with my mother. At the time, I did not speak English, and she barely spoke Spanish, but I felt the meaning of words when she said, "Leave the child alone." She was originally from St. Thomas and eventually moved to St. Croix. At that time the Virgin Islands were under Dutch rule. In 1936 the islands were sold to the US and became the part of the US Virgin Islands. St. Croix is where my mother was born and my grandmother moved to the Dominican Republic when my mother was six months old, looking for work.

At that time, in the early years of the 1900s, the Dominican Republic was frequented by people coming from other islands in search of work. My grandmother taught my mother to sew, embroider, and crochet. At a time when little girls were working, my grandmother managed to send my mother to school. They lived off their sewing and sold doilies door to door. There were times when they did not eat for days, but they would not work in anyone's home. This part of the story I knew. At some point in my life, my mother had shared parts of her childhood with me. What I did not know was what my sister shared with me that night, in the summer of 1985. At that point in my life, I had been married for years and had two children of my own, yet I had not heard this part of the story.

My grandmother was a domestic worker in her native St. Thomas in the late 1800s, one of the few positions open to Black women at that time. While working at this particular household, she had been raped. She was left pregnant, had the child, and when the boy was around three years old, the family kidnapped the boy and sold him to some other family. My grandmother tried for years to recuperate her son, but no one would help her. It took her years to recover him. That was all that was known. She never spoke of how she recovered him. Eventually, she moved to St. Croix, got married, and had my mother. None of us ever knew why she left St. Croix, but she never went back.

This piece of family history put all kinds of things in perspective for me and helped me connect a lot of dots. I flashed back to the day my mother yelled at the woman who was doing the laundry in our backyard, and things began to make sense. Suddenly, I knew why my education was so important to my mother, why I was not allowed to do cleaning or learn to wash clothes. It was more than her trying to keep us from being domestic workers. She was trying to keep us from being raped and perhaps, in her way, trying to save her own mother. When we know the history, we can make sense of the present. History helps us understand people's behavior, connect the dots, and make sense of our world. My mother was clearly traumatized by that story, and my knowing that bit of family history helped me complete that piece of my personal puzzle. My mother experienced many traumas in her life, and despite them, she chose love.

We never know how trauma and continued oppression will manifest. We are all wired differently. This is why someone's treasure is another's burden.

In this book on healing, history is used to understand what we are healing and what we are healing from. Racism is broad and deep. It is steeped in a past that continues to haunt us. It holds the mystery of the missing history and a past we may never come to know.

Racism is a condition created by hundreds of years of conditioning. A condition is a circumstance in which people live and work. Conditioning, according to the Oxford English Dictionary is *"the process of training or accustoming a person or animal to behave in a certain way or to accept certain circumstances."* "Racism is a condition created by hundreds of years of inaccurate learned assumptions and behaviors, or in other words, conditioning." If we want to transform the condition of racism, we have to understand and transform the conditioning. That requires we look at the history that got us to where we are today, and our acceptance of the circumstances caused by what we have been accustomed to accept. As we move through this history, it's important to follow the threads and connect the dots.

As mentioned in the chapter on trauma:

1. Traumatized people traumatize others unless some healing has occurred.

2. You can't traumatize others without you being traumatized.

3. Trauma can be primary or secondary.

4. Trauma gets passed on for up to seven generations.

5. Participating in the traumatization of others compromises your family for generations. That means those beautiful little babies you've not birthed yet will carry your trauma.

If you're going to heal from racism, you need to be trauma-informed.

TRAUMA IN EUROPEAN HISTORY

So let's take a look at Europe in the Middle Ages. It's essential to understand Africans and Europeans had a longstanding history of trade and diplomacy before colonization and enslavement. Let's start in the 1400s; that's when Europeans began traveling to and eventually colonizing the Western Hemisphere. When we look at Europe back in those days, it was a very, very difficult place to live. The monarchy and the papacy were the leaders and often at odds with one another, and everybody else was subservient to them.

They kept people subservient through destabilization, and they were destabilized through violence. So, they had things like the guillotine, which chopped off people's heads. They used the breaking wheel, where they would tie people to a wheel, turn it, and break the prisoner's bones. They would hang (lynch) several people at one time. People were tortured in public. Many would travel for miles to see one beheading or hanging, is called a lynching in the US. Sometimes, there would be five or six people lynched at one time. The problem was it wasn't just the adults watching these spectacles.

The monarchy and the papacy wanted to make sure they stayed in power, and they were just a few people versus the populace. Sometimes a monarchy had thirty family members, including cousins. They had to find a way to control the masses. Violence was quick, efficient, and effective; it traumatized people. Trauma destabilizes, and destabilized people are easy to control.

When people came to see these things, they didn't leave the children home with a babysitter. The adults, the teenagers, the little ones, and the yet-to-be-born were traumatized. Soldiers would force people out of their homes to experience the violence. The idea was to show the villagers what could happen to them or their family, thus making them compliant. Today, as mentioned earlier in this book, we know, through epigenetics, trauma lasts for more than just one lifetime. It remains with the family for generations.

Europe had two economic classes: the nobility and the poor. Among the poor were indentured servants, enslaved Europeans, and the general poor. This included children who were orphaned or abandoned. Sanitation was virtually non-existent. Many diseases resulted from malnutrition and poor sanitation, such as smallpox, cholera, and measles. People were burned to death for saying the wrong thing. Religious persecution was expected, especially for non-Christians.

Food was scarce in Europe's colder climate. Remember from the chapter "Race, Latitude, & Attitude" that people had three, at best five, months to grow their food. Many were malnourished, small, and frail. Because of the cold climate and the short growing season, Europeans had to preserve, count, and measure food supplies to make it last until the next growing season. For the most part, for nine months, Europeans barely saw a leaf on a tree. Many places were cloudy for weeks at a time, creating a feeling of lack and depression. Europe was a difficult place to live. Many were looking for a way out of their desperate conditions.

EARLY EXPLORATION: EUROPE 1400S AND BEYOND

By the 1400s, Portuguese and Spanish explorers traveled through Africa, Asia, and North, Central, and South America. They fought for territory and claimed the wealth found in these countries for their sovereign crown. Their takeover was brutal, as they quickly had to establish rule. They would ride through on horses, using their swords to behead the citizens inhabiting the land. They would steal possessions, rape women, kill children, and burn homes. Those who were left would be tortured and enslaved.

Men like Prince Henry (the Navigator) of Portugal were especially interested in the African continent. While he was neither a navigator nor a sailor as his name suggests, he sponsored many explorations to the African west coast, claiming land and wealth for Portugal. Henry the Navigator is credited with starting the transatlantic slave trade. Prince Henry was not the only one. Many Portuguese and Spanish explorers claimed territory and wealth and enslaved and killed natives wherever they landed. Francisco Vázquez de Coronado traveled more than thirty-five hundred miles looking for gold in what is today's continental United States.

In 1452, the Vatican decreed a papal bull that would change the course of the world forever. It was and is called the Doctrine of Discovery for the Portuguese monarchy. The doctrine would be revised several times, including in 1493, the year Cristóbal Colón (Christopher Columbus) returned to Spain from his expedition to find a new route to India. In 1493, this papal bull, created for Portugal in 1452, was extended to include Spain.

Because the Doctrine of Discovery came from the Vatican, a religious institution created to guide human souls, people took the doctrine as gospel. The Doctrine of Discovery granted legal and spiritual rights to any lands and waterways "discovered" by Christian explorers. This papal bull gave explorers the right to take possession of the lands and waterways and claim them for their sovereign, take the people's possessions, and turn them into perpetual slaves. The doctrine included all they had found would be inherited by their descendants, successors, and heirs.

All European monarchs are related. They intermarried to keep the wealth and power in the family and to create alliances for peace. Word of the Doctrine of Discovery spread to all European nations, and between the 1500s and the 1800s, Africa, Australia, Asia, New Zealand, and North, Central, and South America were colonized. The people inhabiting those lands were forced to give up their land, their language, ways of worshiping, and personal possessions and slavery ensued. And as in their country of old, the colonizers maintained order through extreme violence. The process was to traumatize, destabilize, control.

The Doctrine of Discovery justified and institutionalized colonization globally and the enslavement of native and African people. The doctrine gave Europeans legal, spiritual, and political rights over lands and waterways as long as non-Christians inhabited the lands. This meant Jews, Muslims, Hindus, and Pagans, or any other form of worship familiar and unfamiliar to them. The doctrine gave explorers the right to turn all people into Christians on the lands they took over and establish European rule.

Public whippings, hangings, and various forms of torture were daily rituals. People were quartered, which included tying a person's arms and legs to four different horses and firing a gun to scare the horses and split the person into quarters. Pregnant women were hung by their feet and tied to a tree. Their bellies were cut open, and their babies would suspend by the umbilical cord. The enslaved were made to watch the violence as a warning against running away or revolting.

Trauma can bring on early puberty. As early as eleven years of age, little girls were impregnated by their owners and the owners' friends and family to create more slaves for their masters. Children were sold away from family, worked in the fields as early as age four, and were severely punished for not producing high yields. The children were slaves, which meant they were born without human rights unless their owners allotted rights.

The Doctrine of Discovery has been used throughout time, and it's still alive and well today. In the US alone, the doctrine has been used to resolve land cases. In 1823, the Doctrine of Discovery became part of US law and was used in the case of Johnson v. M'Intosh. In 1830, the doctrine was used to pass the Indian Removal Act, also known as the Trail of Tears, signed into law by President Andrew Jackson. The Indian Removal Act forced Cherokee, Chickasaw, Choctaw, Creek, and Seminole living in the southeastern United States to move to Oklahoma. As of this writing, the last time the Supreme Court used the doctrine was in the year 2005 in the City of Sherrill v. Oneida Indian Nation.

Just as enslaved African and African-American children were separated from their parents by being sold, rented, or given away, Indigenous children were separated by being sent to boarding schools far away from home, a practice Native communities are still healing from today. In his book *Unsettling Truths: The Ongoing, Dehumanizing Legacy of the Doctrine of Discovery*, co-authored by Soong-Chan Rah, Mark Charles describes historical trauma as *"a transgenerational, communal manifestation of PTSD and complex post-traumatic stress disorder (C-PTSD)."* He goes further to explain:

> *On the Navajo Reservation, anyone over the age of fifty is most likely a boarding school survivor who endures the symptoms of PTSD and C-PTSD from that experience. Nearly every Navajo can recall the name and even specific stories about a parent who survived the boarding school or a grandparent or great grandparent who experienced and were even killed during the Long Walk. A generation of elders still reels from the PTSD and C-PTSD of boarding schools while simultaneously struggling with the transgenerational and communal symptoms of HTR from the Long Walk. Repeated complex trauma is being passed down and manifested in the form of historical trauma in the younger generation."*

It's been a long history of traumatic events. Institution-alized racial conditioning has created institutional histori-cal trauma. This has created a culture of people who have normalized the dysfunction of their traumatic history without any social recognition of the trauma and without any healing. We live in a nation that has what Eckhart Tolle, author of *A New Earth*, calls *"the pain body."* America has a huge pain body when it comes to race and racism, a pain body made up of those who have come before us and maintained by those who are living now. And it is this pain body that needs healing. So, how do you heal this pain body? One race literate person at a time.

QUESTIONS TO CONSIDER:

- Did you learn about the Doctrine of Discovery in school?

- Did you study slavery in school?

- How do you feel knowing about this piece of history?

- Where do you feel the Doctrine of Discovery in your body?

- Where do you feel the historical trauma in your body?

CHAPTER 9

HOW RACISM WAS INSTITUTIONALIZED

———

"If the misery of the poor be caused not by the laws of nature, but by our institutions, great is our sin."

—CHARLES DARWIN

LAS CASTAS & THE NEW WORLD

We don't know what we don't know. There is so much history we simply don't learn in school, but what a difference it would make if we did. We are living under a caste system that was established by the Spaniards early into colonization. As soon as Europeans started to colonize various parts of the world, they established social orders based on the same social orders of the countries from which they had migrated. Colonization was done through violence. Killing, looting, burning, and enslavement were the strategies used by Europeans as they took over much of the world. Violence, as mentioned earlier, traumatizes. Trauma destabilizes people, and destabilized people are easier to control. People traveling from Europe were already traumatized by the systemic public violence. Traumatized people traumatize others. Violence was the way to control Indigenous and enslaved populations wherever they landed. Moreover, they had the papal bulls to guide their entitlement. So, they established hierarchical order that put them at the top of the leadership chain.

INSTITUTIONALIZED PARTNERING

The Europeans institutionalized marriage in the new colonies, so the only legal marriages were between a male and female European. That meant all other unions were outside of the institution of marriage and therefore illegal. If you were found to be married outside of your so-called race, you could be jailed or killed. By institutionalizing marriage in this way, it meant any children born outside of the "legal" marriage of two Europeans rendered the birth of Indigenous, Black, and Brown children outside the law or illegal. Those children were called illegitimate. An illegitimate child had no legal rights, so even if they were a man's firstborn male child, they did not have any right to the family wealth. Marriage was institutionalized along racial lines. Whom you could marry was dictated by the state.

To make certain everyone in the society knew their place, the Spaniards created a system called "Las Castas." Las Castas is a pictorial chart outlining social roles and patterns of inheritance, mimicking the European system of firstborn male right to the inheritance. No matter who you mated with, it was made clear to all citizens that the only people who could inherit were the first male child of two Europeans in a legal marriage. That meant a European man could have a child with a native or an African woman, and even if that child was his first male, they could not inherit.

INSTITUTIONALIZED EDUCATION

Las Castas were laid out pictorially because it was illegal for the colonized or enslaved to learn to read and write unless it was in service to the family they were enslaved by. A slave found with a book could be sold, tortured, or killed. The same fate was suffered by natives and, in many cases, White women. This meant the lack of education was institutionalized racially and by gender.

INSTITUTIONALIZED MEDICINE

In my book, *Speaking Race in Healthcare: A Manual for the Dialogue,* I write about racial disparities in health care. Those disparities have a longstanding history. In the early days of colonization, those with power and wealth had access to the health care that was available in their day. However, Indigenous and enslaved people would go to their local healers to be treated for wounds and illnesses. Their relationship with the local healer was based on the trust established over time and through communal bonding. The enslaved community placed more trust on these healers than on the White doctors. The enslaved people knew White doctors and medical students would purchase and rent enslaved men, women, and children to perform medical experiments. Many were killed during those experiments.

One famous doctor was James Marion Sims, known as the father of modern gynecology. He was the president of the American Medical Association in 1876. In 1880, he helped to found and became president of the American Gynecological Society. Brynn Holland, writer for History, the prestigious television channel, writes about Sims in his article entitled "The 'Father of Modern Gynecology' Performed Shocking Experiments on Enslaved Women."

But because Sims' research was conducted on enslaved Black women without anesthesia, medical ethicists, historians, and others say his use of enslaved Black bodies as medical test subjects falls into a long, ethically bereft history that includes the Tuskegee Syphilis Experiment and Henrietta Lacks. Critics say Sims cared more about the experiments than in providing therapeutic treatment, and that he caused untold suffering by operating under the racist notion Black people did not feel pain.

There is a longstanding history of unethical practices in the medical systems that have led Black and Brown people to distrust the medical system. Black bodies were used as subjects of smallpox inoculations (the early form of vaccinations) as early as 1768 in Jamaica. Traditionally, vaccination human trials are often conducted in Africa, Central and South America, Asia, the Caribbean and other poor, Black and Brown communities around the world. Today, between racial disparities, experimentation, and a history that is mostly hidden, People of Color struggle with trust in the health care system.

These are just a few examples of systems that have been institutionalized racially. There is also housing, justice, banking, salary structures, food, environmental racism, and much more. Institutionalizing a nation based on race means large numbers of people are dehumanized. The dehumanized are always underserved, over-accused, exploited, and abused. All of which have a negative impact on Communities of Color and ultimately the nation as a whole.

Think about this: Laws are made by people who either took power by force or to whom we gave our power away. If we are going to take the premise that justice is about balance, then we need people who are balanced to make just laws on our behalf. People are balanced when they understand and see both sides of a problem and can stay as neutral as possible. When people receive partial truths and colorful myths, such as the myth of race and supremacy, they become emotionally, mentally, physically, or spiritually imbalanced, or some combination thereof. Moreover, people who carry unhealed trauma tend to be imbalanced in the area of their lives afflicted by that trauma.

To put it in plain words, sick people make laws that make the whole society sick. The Doctrine of Discovery took an already suffering world and made it sicker. And by looking to hold some of its people in bondage, it enslaved us all to centuries of fear and violence.

Understanding where all this institutionalized racism was established can be helpful in creating a treatment plan that helps heal the entire global community. If we are going to heal, we need to understand what we are really dealing with. Humans are resilient beings with an extraordinary power to heal and transform.

QUESTIONS TO CONSIDER:

- How was racism institutionalized?

- How do laws steeped in racial conditioning affect us today?

- Can you give examples of laws that are racially based?

- How does it affect us to live in a nation where the law-makers are racially unaware?

- What needs to change?

CHAPTER 10

RECONSTRUCTION & BEYOND

"Prisoners bound with heavy chains for years, starved and emaciated, weak and exhausted, and with eyes so long cast down in darkness they remember not the light, do not leap up in joy the instant they are made free. It takes a while for them to understand what freedom is."

—*A COURSE IN MIRACLES*

REPARATIONS

We can't speak about race without mentioning reparations. On January 1, 1863, President Abraham Lincoln signed the Emancipation Proclamation, which declared *"all persons held as slaves are, and henceforward shall be free."* However, a lesser-known fact is according to the National Archives, *"Lincoln signed a bill in 1862 that paid up to three hundred dollars for every enslaved person freed"* in the District of Columbia Compensated Emancipation Act. The compensation went to slave owners who were loyal to the Union during the Civil War, not the freed slaves. Note the slave owners in Washington, DC, were compensated for the loss of labor before the Emancipation was proclaimed. The District of Columbia Emancipation Act also included *"voluntary colonization of former slaves to locations outside the United States, and payments of up to one hundred dollars for each person choosing emigration."*

How does one begin to make reparations? From the 1400s, European monarchs, with the help of the Catholic Church, fought, looted, killed, colonized, extracted free labor, stole land, and extracted natural resources from lands that were not theirs. They left the people in poverty, treated humans as cargo, and exported them as goods to other lands. How does one begin to assess the damage and the cost in finances and human suffering? And then, how does one repair it? Reparations is about fixing and making things right again, repairing what has been damaged. The financial compensation owed to the colonized and enslaved, their descendants, successors, and heirs, is immeasurable. The amount owed is in capital, natural resources, human labor, and human lives. Even after enslaved Americans were set free, the toll exacted on them continued.

After the Civil War, many of the newly freed enslaved moved north to work in the factories of New York, New Jersey, Philadelphia, and Chicago. Used to the hard labor and long hours of slave labor, many Jewish families employed African-Americans in their homes and factories. While the South was still reeling from the trauma of the war that was mostly fought on their doorsteps, the rest of the country was becoming industrialized.

But the Jim Crow laws, and the newly arrived Europeans once again took precedence over the experienced Black Americans (then called Negroes). They were used to train the newly arrived, and then they were let go, forcing them into poverty. Many went back south to stay with family. So, what were Jim Crow laws?

> *Jim Crow laws were a collection of state and local statutes that legalized racial segregation. Named after a Black minstrel show character, the laws—which existed for about one hundred years, from the post-Civil War era until 1968—were meant to marginalize African-Americans by denying them the right to vote, hold jobs, get an education, or other opportunities. Those who attempted to defy Jim Crow laws often faced arrest, fines, jail sentences, violence, and death* (Jim Crow Laws, HISTORY 2018, 2021).

This was a time when the KKK made its presence known throughout the South. A Black person's life was only worth the labor it could produce. Black men, women, and children were hunted and hung for sport, and many were accused of false crimes to have the entertainment of a nighttime picnic, known as a lynching. Just like families, including children, showed up in Europe for hangings and beheadings, they would show up in the US in mass for a lynching. And even though the average White person may not have known about the Doctrine of Discovery or remember the terror and horror of ancient Europe, the reality of those past lives was in their bones. The rush of seeing a person publicly tortured for sport was not part of the "New World."

Then there were the riots. In my seminars, I give partici-pants a phrase and ask them to tell me the people's race that came to mind. Try this yourself as you read this. The phrase is "race riot." Who (and by "who" I mean what color people) comes to mind as you think of the words "race riot?" Every time I would ask this question in my seminars, participants, regardless of their skin color, would respond, "Black people." Their response showed a lack of awareness of history.

Before the civil rights movement, race riots consisted of White people in mass destroying, burning, and looting Black homes, businesses, and communities as well as terrorizing and killing its citizens. Kidnapping children, arresting innocent men and women, accusing them of crimes the Whites had committed, and leaving communities to rebuild on their own with no city assistance was part of the way these riots worked. The summer of 1919 was known as "Red Summer" because there were so many such riots across the US. White people would destroy Black communities because they were angry the people in those communities were prospering in spite of Jim Crow laws. Such was the case in Tulsa, Oklahoma, in 1921.

On May 31, 1921, *"during the Tulsa Race Massacre (also known as the Tulsa Race Riot), which occurred over eighteen hours on May 31 to June 1, 1921, a White mob attacked residents, homes, and businesses in the predominantly Black Greenwood neighborhood of Tulsa, Oklahoma. The event remains one of the worst incidents of racial violence in US history."* Most of these riots never made it to the history books. As a result, when you tell someone to picture a race riot, most people will think of Black people. The reason for that is people often think of the riots that happened after Dr. Martin Luther King, Jr. was murdered, and other more recent riots that have made the news and the history books.

On January 6, 2021, in plain view of the entire world, a White mob attacked the US Capitol, looking for politicians to hang, spurred on by the newly deposed president of the United States. Not even half of the insurrectionist terrorists have been caught and punished. Most were simply allowed to walk back to their hotels in Washington, DC, go through airport security, and fly home to resume their normal lives after the riot. And while the president himself was impeached (for the second time) for inciting the riot, there were not enough members of his party in the Senate to vote to impeach him. You'll understand why when we look at supremacy in the chapter "Who Internalized the Caste System?" in this book.

If we are going to understand the present, we will need to look at our past. There is no other way forward. We have already tried ignoring the past and look at where it's gotten us.

QUESTIONS TO CONSIDER:

- Were you educated about our racial history in school?

- Do you believe it's important for students to learn accurate history?

- Do you believe racial myth is a healthy way to protect children?

- Are you open to becoming race literate?

- Can we consider reparations outside of the Doctrine of Discovery?

CHAPTER 11

THE FIVE LEVELS OF RACIAL CONDITIONING

———

"Out of your vulnerabilities will come your strength."
—SIGMUND FREUD

Over the years, I've seen individuals and organizations look to solve racism as if it were a headache. Take a pill, go to bed, and it will be done in the morning. Time after time, I've watched organizations call what is to me a racial incident a "diversity issue." Their way of handling it? "Let's do diversity training, that way everyone feels included." Racism can't be managed by inclusion tactics. Yes, inclusion is needed, but racism is so much more than that. Racism is institutional, systemic, internalized, personal, and interpersonal. Let's unpack it by looking at it through the lens of the five levels of racial conditioning.

RACISM IS INSTITUTIONAL

When it comes to institutionalized racism, one has to consider who establishes laws, who makes the rules, whom the rules are made to protect, and whom the rules are made to control.

We institutionalize something by turning it into law. Laws are the ways ideologies become the rules we must all follow. These rules govern and control the ways people behave in a society. Some examples of things that have been institutionalized are land, housing, education, medicine, punishment, money, food, transport, marriage, and much more. If we don't follow the rules institutionalized in society, there are consequences. It is fear of the consequences— physical, such as torture or incarceration, and emotional, such as regret, guilt, and shame—that keep people in line. Convenience and the promise of peace and order are among the many reasons people accept the systems of their country. Without the acceptance of the people, the institutions cannot stand.

Race was institutionalized hundreds of years ago as a way to justify the human resource of unpaid labor supplied by people trafficked from the African continent. Melanin, the color pigmentation that darkens the skin of people whose biological tribes developed close to the equator, was used as the marker of human worth and deservability. Here are some examples of what has been institutionalized racially and how.

LAND – NATIONAL LAND TRUST

If you want to understand how land ownership was institutionalized, you need to look no further than Native/Indigenous land laws anywhere that was colonized by a European country. Those whose families were living on lands inhabited by their ancestors for millennia lost their rights to that land through the Doctrine of Discovery.

The Doctrine is an international law institutionalized by the papacy, 1452 to 1493, that is still being used today. You can learn more about the Doctrine of Discovery in this book's History chapter. If you live in Africa, Australia, Asia, New Zealand, and North, Central, and South America, you are living under the sovereign law of the Doctrine of Discovery.

HOUSING – HUD

In the US alone, the GI Bill made housing loans available to soldiers coming back from the Second World War. A US soldier, who had served honorably and fought for global freedom, had the right to housing mortgage at the lowest interest rates in history. Less than 2 percent of those loans went to Black soldiers and Soldiers of Color. Although they had fought honorably and valiantly, some of their units even decorated for their brave service, the GI Bill did not apply to them.

Housing was segregated and organized racially. Houses were valued higher if they were in a White neighborhood than a neighborhood where People of Color lived. The housing market for Blacks and People of Color was, for the most part, a rental market. Rentals only build equity for those who own the property, and most properties were owned by White people. This meant People of Color could not build equity from real estate. They could not pass their homes on to the next generation.

In the meantime, White people were using the equity from their homes to pass on wealth to their offspring, using it to pay for their children's education, their first home, building businesses, and accumulating wealth.

From getting a mortgage to getting a business loan to paying higher insurance premiums to getting paid less for their labor, Black people and People of Color have always been on the losing end of the economic war.

While institutionally, White people were targeted to be invested in, by law, Black people and People of Color were being divested of their wealth. Their labor has been traditionally unpaid or underpaid. According to the National Fund for Workforce Solutions, *"White workers with a high school diploma and no college [earn nineteen dollars per hour], and Black workers with an associate's degree [eighteen dollars per hour]. Racial inequities in income cost the US economy about 2.3 trillion dollars per year"* (Langston, Scoggins, and Walsh, 2020).

The gap is much larger when you compare wages by race and gender. For every dollar a White man makes, a Black man makes eighty-seven cents. Native Americans and Hispanics/Latinos make ninety-one cents. While Asian men earn more than White men, they are not treated equally in the workplace and face other forms of discrimination. For every dollar a White man earns, White women make seventy-nine cents, and Black women sixty-two cents. Hispanics/Latinas are paid fifty-four cents, Native women fifty-seven, and Asian women ninety cents.

And the differences break down even further. Research has found the darker a person's skin is, the less they earn, with lighter skin Blacks earning higher wages than their darker skin colleagues, as mentioned previously in this book.

Whiteness is not just a skin color; it is a privilege bestowed upon certain individuals. For instance, at the beginning of the twentieth century, the US had many classifications of race pertaining to Europeans, especially Eastern Europeans. When the Irish and the Italians started arriving in the US in the late 1800s and the early 1900s, they were not considered White. In their case, having White skin did not afford any privilege. They had to assimilate, lose their accent, or stop speaking their native language to assimilate. But eventually, they could assimilate. Assimilation was important because it meant privilege. Privilege made it easier to get a job. With your basic needs taken care of, you could create a life in America. Then you had to protect that privilege; that meant not allowing others in, namely Black and Brown people. Protecting the privilege of whiteness maintains the system of White supremacy firmly. Privilege, in the case of race, refers to access and opportunity based on having White skin. It is a privilege based on a color caste system founded on supremacy.

EDUCATION

Education has long been seen as the way out of poverty and limitations in the Black communities and Communities of Color. These people took and continue to take great pride in educating themselves and their children. But education costs money. In the US, public schools are funded by the tax dollars a community contributes. If your property is undervalued, the workers in the community are underpaid, the effects of that show up in the schools. Books, extracurricular activities, tutoring, and even mentoring are affected.

MEDICINE UNDER THE FDA

Medicine is one of the great institutions of our nation. But good medical care costs money. One of the ways higher education has sought to balance racial disparity in medical care has been to build university hospitals in underserved neighborhoods.

From the outside looking in, this arrangement looks like a win-win. But sometimes, the community has looked upon these hospitals, filled with White medical students who are filled with their own racial conditioning, with suspicion and disdain.

The institution of medicine has used Black and Brown bodies as subjects of experiments for a very long time. Since the times of slavery, when doctors would rent enslaved persons to experiment on, from the Tuskegee Syphilis Experiments to testing vaccines on South and Central American, Caribbean, and African citizens, the Black and Brown community often distrusts the institution of medicine.

COURTS

Some African-Americans refer to the institution of laws as "just-us," namely justice for White people.

America is a country of laws. The problem is laws do not always equate to justice. Justice is a return to balance. Laws are rules to be followed with consequences for those who do not. However, the law is not applied equally across the board. One example is the disproportionate ways in which Blacks get arrested for drug crimes compared to White people. According to the American Civil Liberties Union (ACLU), *"nationwide, the arrest data revealed one consistent trend: significant racial bias. Despite roughly equal usage rates, Blacks are 3.73 times more likely than Whites to be arrested for marijuana."*

FOOD – FDA

Where supermarkets, farmers markets, and fast food restaurants are placed have little to do with Black and Brown people. While working on Congressional Conversations on Race, a program that worked with several members of Congress and their constituents to craft a race conversation that allowed all sides to be heard, we worked with a member whose district was in the middle of a food desert. A food desert is a neighborhood that has few if any supermarkets and little to no access to fresh fruits and vegetables. These neighborhoods often have several fast food places on one block.

To address this, I had recommended a process which had proven successful in my programs. We met with the member of Congress who had invited us and his staff to determine what area of race he wanted to focus on. Among several topics, he wanted to focus on the food deserts in his district. We took the member of Congress and his colleagues, including council members and leaders of the top three supermarkets in his district, on a historical tour and included the food desert and the area where the farmers market met on a weekly basis.

As it happened, the farmers market was outside of the Black neighborhood. And while there was a bus in the neighborhood, there was no bus stop anywhere near the farmers market. While on the bus, one of the council members made a call from her cell phone. She then announced that as of the next day, there would be a bus stopping at the farmers market and it would be a regular bus stop from then on.

After the tour, we engaged in a conversation with the citizens, some local farmers who participated in the discussion, and the supermarkets represented. They agreed to continue the conversations after we left. At the time, all seemed eager to find a way forward and create a way to make fresh fruits and vegetables available to the community. People can work together toward change. Awareness and the willingness to face reality are essential to healing.

While many things can be institutionalized, there's always the reality that we cannot legislate people's hearts. And people's hearts are what need to change if we are to heal from racism.

ECOLOGY

We have institutionalized ecological/environmental safety, but in spite of these laws, Black and Brown communities disproportionately suffer environmental racism. Landfills, toxic waste sites, and industrial activity with their noise and pollution not only disrupt physical health, but they can also cause mental distress. Such sites are found in financially disadvantaged areas, and usually, those areas house People of Color. Across the board, racism impacts all our institutions.

RACISM IS SYSTEMIC

Systems are set up to support what is institutionalized. Examples of those systems are:

- Food and Drug Administration (FDA)

- Policing system – Law enforcement, public safety

- Court/Judicial system

- Housing system – United States Department of Housing and Urban Development (HUD)

- Medical/health care system

- Transportation system

We have systems that govern airwaves, radio waves, and microwaves. All of these are under laws that are meant to protect all equally. But as we look closer, we find the systems set up to uphold the laws are filled with racial disparities. Just as the institutions that created these systems to uphold their laws suffer from racial conditioning and the people who co-create the laws are afflicted, so are the systems and the people who work in these systems.

RACISM IS INTERNALIZED

People born, living, and working under these systems internalize what is institutionalized, accepting it as "just the way things are," and they act out of what is in their environment. They police their neighbors even when, in their hearts, they know it's wrong. The behavior becomes rote; we call this unconscious behavior, stemming from internalized biases from living in a racialized system. People internalize what they experience. They also internalize repeated actions and reactions, and they then interact out of what has been learned, which they now believe to be normal. The dysfunction becomes normalized.

I remember a friend of mine told me about a couple he was friends with. They had arrived from Eastern Europe a few years prior, and the only place they could afford to live was in a Black neighborhood in New York City. He said his friends seemed comfortable there and even made some friends in the neighborhood. About two years later, the husband got a very good paying job. His wife did not need to work anymore, and they moved to the suburbs. About another year after he got his job, he was sent on an assignment to the same neighborhood where they had lived when he first arrived. He said he couldn't believe he had lived there because he was now afraid of the neighborhood and its people. At that point, he had been in the country for about four years.

RACISM IS PERSONAL

Because racism is internalized, it becomes unconscious. People do and say racist things without conscious awareness of what they are doing; this is what we call implicit racism or implicit bias because, as a culture, we have normalized the dysfunction of racism. We try to compensate with political correctness, but not saying the wrong thing is different from not thinking it and not feeling it. Racism makes it natural for White people to see themselves as more efficient than People of Color. As a result, they make what seem like non-offensive comments in their interactions with People of Color that Black and Brown people find offensive and call them out as racist.

RACISM IS INTERPERSONAL

People can't help but act, react, and interact with each other out of what they have internalized. What is in the environment is what they know. During times of slavery, Native Americans owned enslaved Africans and their descendants. Free Black Americans owned Black slaves. Europeans owned White slaves, and in fact, the first slaves in America were European slaves brought over by other Europeans on their voyages to the Americas. What we internalize becomes personal, and we act out of what is personal to us.

In Germany, during the Second World War, neighbors turned in neighbors because they were Jewish. Some were themselves Jews. During slavery, people turned in those who planned to run away. When the dysfunction becomes normalized, there is an undercurrent of fear that runs through the population. People fear and thereby distrust one another. When the dysfunction becomes normalized, no one is safe.

Today, interpersonal racism shows up as macro- and microaggressions between coworkers. It shows up at Starbucks when a White woman working there calls the police because two Black men are sitting at a table waiting for a colleague. Interpersonal racism is Amy Cooper calling the police to say a Black man (who videotaped the incident) was attacking her when all he did was ask her to put her dog on a leash. Interpersonal racism shows up in the relationship of the police in Black and Brown neighborhoods.

Let's break down the subtle ways we learn racism from our circle of influence, as seen through the five levels of racial conditioning.

PERSONAL

Personal racism is what we carry within ourselves, having learned it from our circle of influence. The personal level is where implicit and explicit biases are stored. And it is the first place we go for information about racism.

OUR FAMILY – INTERPERSONAL

We are as much affected by what our parents say as we are by what they don't. When it comes to racism, silence is deadly. Those who grow up to run the systems have the life of those they serve in the palms of their hands. How they choose to interpret the laws handed down by our institutions is made with a lifetime of conditioning. Conditioning that starts at home is reinforced by those who care for the family.

PEERS – INTERPERSONAL

Friends, classmates, and even strangers have the power to influence us. Our peers decide if we are popular or shunned. The desire to belong is strong in humans. Without a strong sense of self, people will do anything to belong. The groups we belong to, whom we have as friends, the people who come over for dinner, are often the same people our parents had over for dinner. They look the same, act the same, have the same basic socioeconomic background, and even sound the same.

COMMUNITY – INTERPERSONAL/SYSTEMIC/INSTITUTIONAL

Our community is not just made up of the people who surround us; it is also made up of our housing, schools, and parishes. Our community is influenced by the beliefs of the people who inhabit it. For hundreds of years, America has lived in chosen and eventually institutionalized segregation through Jim Crow laws—separate but equal. White people have been led to believe the world was equal for all. They've believed we all have equal rights; we are all treated with the same respect, and have had the same freedoms as they have. That myth, or the desire to believe that myth, has led to a lot of poverty, pain, and even death to People of Color while White people remained silent.

POLITICS – INSTITUTIONAL

Politicians have always used the myth of race to their advantage. Pitting people against each other, they have used racist ideology to maintain the status quo and to keep themselves in power. The reason politicians could run and win on a platform of racial division is that Americans, by the time they reach voting age, have had a lifetime of racial conditioning. So, their racial condition becomes a pawn in a dangerous game of political chess. They have moved around from here to there as they become more and more detached from the global village, a village that is made up of seventy percent People of Color.

EDUCATION – SYSTEMIC

A system that has been institutionalized racially that segregates history and teaches partial truths sets its students up to maintain the myth of race. But that doesn't change the fact that it is not real. There are no genetic markers differentiating one group of humans from another. People have melanin in their skin to protect them from the harsh sun that warms our planet. Those whose tribes have lived in cold climates where there is very little sun lose the melanin of their African ancestors. Scientists estimate that it takes approximately twenty thousand years for what was once "Black skin" to become "White skin." All hair is protein. The difference between hair texture—straight hair, wavy, curly, or the super tight curls of African people is the follicle, which is the little hole that the hair comes through. In fact, straight hair, according to 23and Me, is one of the traits left over from the Neanderthals.

MEDIA – INSTITUTIONAL

The media has been known to make or break presidents, and it has played its share of a role in perpetuating and maintaining the myth of race. From daily newspapers to magazine covers, from movies to cartoons, the images we see as children and experience through our life leave an indelible mark that becomes part of our beliefs, perceptions, and expectations. Media holds a great deal of power, and therefore a great deal of responsibility in the ways that it perpetuates the myth of race and the reality of racism.

RELIGION – INSTITUTIONAL

We live in a nation that separates church and state. However, we are under sovereign, international law, dictated by a papal bull, created in the Vatican between 1452 and 1493, known as the Doctrine of Discovery. Religion has also served to keep racism in place, from the Doctrine of Discovery to the Christian schools native children were forced to attend. From the holding and selling of enslaved Africans and their descendants to the slave catechisms, religion has held a central post in maintaining segregation and racism in place. As a result, there are Black churches and White churches, both preaching unity while maintaining their distance.

PHYSICAL ENVIRONMENT – INSTITUTIONAL/ SYSTEMIC/INTERPERSONAL/INTERNALIZED

As children, we are subconsciously influenced by our physical environment, and we absorb it like sponges. What is in the air of our nation gets absorbed like an invisible gas that permeates our psyche. Race is a myth that conditions us into the very painful and very real condition of racism and weakens our humanity.

The role of healing is to help us understand that we can't help but be racially conditioned by the racist institutions and systems we live under. And unless we become conscious of our conditioning, we will consciously and unconsciously act, react, and interact with one another out of the racism we have internalized, the racial trauma we have experienced and inherited, and the colorism we have learned from living in a racialized system. As we grow, that absorption becomes the foundation of our beliefs, and it becomes hardwired into our personalities. This is how we are indoctrinated into racism. Then we act, react, and interact out of what we have absorbed.

By the time children are three years old, they have been indoctrinated into their respective racial class, and the rest of their lives are spent consciously and unconsciously being fed by a system that castes racism unless there's intervention. Intervention happens through education grounded in race literacy, compassion, and wholeness.

When it comes to racism, it seems like everyone wants to solve it at the interpersonal level without understanding how racism was internalized. These are what Henry David Thoreau would call the branches rather than the roots. The roots of racism are grounded in the institutional, supported by the systemic, and filtered through our circle of influence, generation after generation.

Racism is very personal. We, as human beings, are more than flesh and bone. We are extraordinary! We are creatures of change, and when it comes to racism, that change can happen very fast. But you can't just engage the head. To heal, we must be willing to engage the heart. We are limited in how much we can legislate people's behavior. We have had civil rights laws for more than fifty years. But macro- and microaggressions and violence against Black and Brown people have not stopped. If we don't work on the internalized, interpersonal racism will never change. We cannot legislate people's hearts.

To heal racism, we need to become conscious we are dealing with one problem that has been internalized in different forms by different people. Racism has been institutionalized in a variety of forms and affects us based on where we fall in the caste system. While institutions need to take a long hard look at how laws, policies, and procedures, most of which have been created by White people, affect People of Color, there is more work to be done. If we are going to solve racism, we have to look at the internalized/personal side of our racial dysfunction while working to dismantle it at the institutional level. Ultimately, institutions are made up of people, and if those people continue to function from their internalized racial conditioning, they will continue to make racist policies that negatively affect People of Color. In the end, those who are misinformed are bound to miscreate.

QUESTIONS TO CONSIDER:

- Does it help you to understand racism from the five levels of conditioning?

- Would you be able to explain the five levels to others?

- Are you starting to see racism is learned conditioning?

- Have you ever acted out of your racial conditioning? If so, in what ways?

CHAPTER 12

DOING GOOD DEEDS

––––––

THE TENNIS STORY

Being conscious means being aware of our choices and how those choices affect ourselves and others. It isn't always about what we do, but how what we do affects others.

I remember a friend who helped restore a tennis club in a non-White section of a major city in the eastern US. As a White male with access to wealth, my friend was able to raise the money needed to get the work done and get the place fully operational. Before he and his good intentions made an appearance, this once rundown building served the community as an afterschool tennis center, but my friend turned it into a state-of-the-art tennis club. Young people had a place to go after school, and my friend was proud of what he had done. So proud, in fact, he mentioned his pride often in conversations to the woman who ran the after-school club for the children.

One day, the woman who ran the club got very angry with him and told him she was sick of his bragging. *"After all,"* she snapped at him, *"we would have done this for our children if we had access to the money.*" My friend was angry, insulted, and told me how ungrateful she was, *"after all he had done for that club,"* this was how he was being repaid, with her anger.

In his innocence or ignorance, he had not considered what it must have been like for the parents of those children who would love to have restored the place themselves but felt helpless by virtue of not having access to the financial resources that would have given them the ability to restore the club.

My friend did not realize by "doing it for them" and not involving the community in the process as equal partners who brought their talent, time, and vision to the table, he was once again telling them they were not equal. He was unconsciously putting out the message their talent and labor were nothing next to the cash and access to wealth he brought. This was not an ill-intended man. He genuinely wanted to help. But when we value money more than we do relationships, and we are dealing with people who value relationships over money, we will always have an imbalance.

He was once again "putting them in their place," where what they had to give (talent, labor, creativity, and time) was perceived as not as valuable as the money invested in the project. Had he valued their input as much as his own, he would have seen the equivalent value of what they had to offer. He would have seen their involvement was as important as the money to help rebuild the club.

Why is it we have such a hard time translating talent, labor, and time into dollars and cents when we are dealing with people who have fewer dollars and cents than others? Perhaps what the woman at the club wanted was for the children, who would now be using the newly renovated club, to see their own community contributing to the renovations. They had been running the children's tennis club before he came. They simply did not have money to invest in the renovation project.

If access to wealth is dependent on talent and hard work, then those who are talented and hardworking would have wealth as a result of their daily contributions. By the same token, those who do not work as hard as the man or woman who works from dawn to dusk should not have the wealth of the world at his or her feet. Access to wealth is not always something that is earned. Some come to it through the simple act of birth. We live in a world where equality is relative.

Those who do not experience racial discrimination as part of their life's repertoire do not have a platform from which to understand the unconscious or hidden meanings behind the actions and reactions of those with a different framework unless someone with the experience explains it to them. This is why we need to come together to heal in the community. It's true on a given project, not all contributors are equal, but one can surely see all contributors have value. In a world where people are angry with a playing field that has never been equal, we need to be conscious of the motives behind our actions.

My friend is a man with a kind and giving heart who genuinely wants to make a positive difference. Without the background to understand the depth of this woman's comment, all we can feel is the sting of ingratitude. Without historical information, we lack the ability and miss the opportunity to understand the subtle dynamics of the messages behind our actions. History gives us the context that allows us to have a more accurate picture of the situation.

When we don't involve those whom we are looking to help, we put forth an energy that says we are not all equal contributors to this project. Had he considered the talents to be as valuable as the money, he would have entered into partnership with the community members from the very beginning of the project. An action of that sort tells all, including the self, that my human-family-sibling is my equal, and although what they have to offer is not the same, it is as valuable as the cash I bring. That action would have gone a longer way to healing than rebuilding the club and handing it over for them to use. He did not understand that to the woman, his actions said, "You are not my equal." If equality is measured by financial means, as it often is in our country, she was not in a position to measure up.

The more we live out of our wholeness, the more we see others as our equals.

The thing to remember is equal does not mean the same. By divine right, we are all equal, but in order to encompass wholeness as a world, we are not all the same. We each offer different gifts to our world. This is not because we don't inwardly possess all the gifts, but because, as physical beings, we believe ourselves to be limited in the expression of these gifts.

Even science cannot dispute the fact that within each and every one of us is a part of something greater, that there is something so unique and wonderful we don't yet understand. Biologically we are all related, as has been shown by the Human Genome Project, which traced the human race to a woman in Africa. The HGP was a research project conducted by an international group of researchers looking to map and sequence the all the genes of Homo sapiens. The project was started in 1990 and completed in 2003. They used the mitochondrial DNA, which men and women have, but only the women pass it on. In a way, mitochondrial DNA is the thread that connects us all as a human family. According to many spiritual teachings, we are all related, children of the same source, spiritual siblings. Perhaps if we look at life through the eyes of the larger picture, we can see the truth of our sibling rivalry.

The gift of variety is the gift of unity. We each offer a different ingredient to the global pie, but because nothing we do is ever done in isolation, each individual contribution affects us all. If those with the financial means saw those with talent who do not have access to the wealth as their equal, they would be able to form partnerships that would enhance our world. There would be an honoring of what each one brings to the table that would change our world. I can't make a pie if all I have is sugar. But if I bring my sugar and you bring your flour, and another sibling brings the fruits, and so on…we can have the ingredients to make something delicious happen. Equal does not mean the same, but it does mean we are interdependent. It does mean your ingredients are just as valuable as mine and together we can create a whole that is greater than the sum of its parts.

Beyond all this bantering, there is a simple truth, one that is so obvious we can no longer hide from it. Equality is not equity. The parents of the children in the tennis club did not have equal access.

Supremacy often blinds White people. Their access and opportunity lead them to perform acts of goodness for Communities of Color that these communities would do for themselves if they had access to the money.

QUESTIONS TO CONSIDER:

- Where are you being the racial knight in shining armor?

- Where are you racially imposing your will?

- Are you a Person of Color who resents White rescue?

- How would your life change with greater access to opportunity?

CHAPTER 13

BRINGING THE UNCONSCIOUS TO LIGHT

———

"No person is your friend who demands your silence or denies your right to grow."

—ALICE WALKER

Comedian George Carlin once offered a great line in one of his comedy routines, joking about how to get out of jury duty. He said, *"I'd make a great juror because I can spot a guilty person, just like that."* In many ways, we live our lives in the jury box of individual and collective judgment. Judging with only part of the story can create circumstances and expectations that keep us stagnant. By not considering the natural curiosity that is basic to human nature, we miss out on the valuable information others might share if we only dare to sit and have a conversation. Judgments keep us repeating patterns that are part of our past conditioning. The familiarity of these patterns creates the illusion we are safe in our judgments.

Science tells us we are one human family, joined together by our collective DNA. Science also tells us if you separate a tissue donor from their DNA sample, whatever affects the donor through external stimuli also affects the tissue sample (the DNA). In the book *Awakening to Zero Point*, Gregg Braden cites an experiment conducted by the US military during WWII in which tissue was taken from the mouth of a donor. The donor was given external stimuli through a variety of visual images projected on a screen. The images included sad films, erotic films, and comedies, all to elicit emotions from the donor. The researchers found the DNA had the same reaction as the donor at precisely the same time as the donor. They kept moving the DNA sample farther away from the donor with no change in the experiment. The experiment was stopped at fifty miles.

Think of the implications of this research. A member of our family can be affected by what we think, even when we have not said a word. Moreover, each and every one of us is affected by what the other thinks. Think of what it means to have a whole group of people thought of as the "good guys" by our society and imagine the implications to those who are seen in a bad light.

Our DNA traces the entire human race, as it exists today, to one single source: the remains of one woman in Africa. *"The made-for-cable documentary film* The Real Eve *is predicated on the theory the human race can be traced to a common ancestor. The mitochondrial DNA of one prehistoric woman, who lived in Africa, has according to this theory been passed down from generation to generation over a span of one hundred fifty thousand years."* This documentary, *The Real Eve*, directed by Andrew Piddington and narrated by actor Danny Glover, looked at people's DNA from various parts of the globe and compared their samples to find African-Americans,

Polynesians, Europeans, Asians, Indians, and Native Americans all had DNA from this one woman in Africa.

If this holds true, we could very well be carrying not just the experiences of our current circumstances, but the collective joys and fears of our biological family, as well as that of the entire human race, from the beginning of time. Our cells literally carry the memory of every celebration, every ritual, every invention, every war, every torture, every holocaust, every discovery, every genocide, every famine, every lynching, every humiliation, every act of bravery, every cowardly act, and every act of kindness that has ever transpired on Earth. Along with that, we may also be carrying the emotions or the effects of the emotions that accompanied each of these circumstances and acts.

We have often said what affects one affects us all. The implications of this work could be phenomenal in helping us understand collective patterns of addiction to our racial conditioning and our inability to solve the race issue. On the other hand, think of what a change of mind and heart could do to resolve this same issue. Our thoughts of peace and unity are also transmitted over our "human DNA broadcasting system." Think of the implications that getting out of denial and facing ourselves as we really are can have on our global human family. Even more important, think of what creating new patterns of behavior founded on the principles of genuine equity can do for our globe.

"You cannot get through a single day without having an impact on the world around you. What you do makes a difference, and you have to decide what kind of difference you want to make."
—JANE GOODALL

We can't make a difference while we are in denial. Denial is one of those things that keep us from moving forward. One of the things I had to face was how I denied how racism hurts White people. In my own ignorance, I saw them as the recipients of the unearned privileges their status gave them. As I delved deeper, I began to see how privilege makes oppression invisible for White people. I saw how the threat of being isolated from their peers leads them to collude in a dehumanizing conspiracy of silence that keeps them trapped in the same cycle of violence they perpetrate or allow. It is a violence that has come back to hurt the very communities they have sought to protect at the hands of their own community members. And the silence means we never speak about White-on-White crime unless it's a mass shooting, which further fuels the problem.

As Dr. Martin Luther King, Jr. said in his letter from Birmingham Jail, *"Injustice anywhere is a threat to justice everywhere."*

The stumbling block to getting to this place of healthy self-expression is it takes honest self-assessment and a genuine desire to move from the pain of victimization, guilt, and shame to a place of internal peace and self-empowerment. In other words, we have to move beyond the pain of our past to get there. Of course, it is not necessary to face every agonizing detail of our past human existence, bringing us to this moment. But it's important to look at enough of the truth to get us each to see how we collude with a system of dysfunction that does not serve us as individuals or our planet as a whole.

We live most of our lives out of unconscious patterns of behavior, but once those patterns are brought to conscious awareness, the pattern is no longer this obscure thing that has power over us. Awareness of the pattern gives us a choice, and we can choose to begin the process of dismantling it. While we walk blindly through a life of privilege or oppression, we are condemned through our denial to uphold the very thing we are looking to heal from. The privilege could be as simple as not having to ever worry about racial profiling or not having to worry about whether your local school children have access to technology by having enough computers in their classrooms. The privilege could be as simple as believing the sky really is the limit for you while demanding those who have been left hopeless and without boots pull themselves up by their own bootstraps. The life-filters of having always had socks and boots allows one to believe others have always had the same, or perhaps that is what we need to convince ourselves of in order to stay sane.

Healing from racism is about becoming conscious, awake, and aware. It is about bringing the unconscious to light and grappling with the pain and discomfort. It is about judging and blaming less often and taking greater responsibility for our own thoughts, feelings, and behaviors. Healing is about understanding our sacred connection to one another. There is one thread that has joined us together throughout time. We are one human family.

QUESTIONS TO CONSIDER:

- How do you bring your unconscious to light?

- What part of the healing journey do you find most ominous?

- When it comes to race and racism, what are you in denial about?

- What makes the journey into wholeness difficult?

- Where are your pitfalls?

CHAPTER 14

WHO INTERNALIZED THE CASTE SYSTEM?

"A thief judges by his own conditions."

—ELZEIRA ROBBINS, MY GRANDMOTHER

When I was about five years old, my sister, who was in her early thirties, left the Dominican Republic to live in New York City with her young daughter. My sister loved fashion, having spent most of her life as a seamstress in our country. She sent me this beautiful sky-blue dress. It had a fitted bodice, and the skirt had three layers of finely pleated Georgette fabric with a hem of lace at the bottom. It was beautiful! I couldn't wait to wear it! My mother let me wear it one Sunday, and I felt like a princess in it.

That afternoon, one of the children known as the policemen's kids (the White children in the neighborhood) came by my backyard. It was strange because those children never played or even spoke to me. She stared at my dress and said, *"Beautiful dress, except for the color of your skin."* I felt sick to my stomach, embarrassed and ashamed. I never told my parents. In school, when kids were picking teams, I never got picked, despite being really good in sports. The teacher would always have to assign me to a team. Light-skinned Dominicans felt they were better than dark-skinned Dominicans and made no bones about it, especially the girls and women. I spent a great deal of time angry at their ignorance until I started healing and understood the history had been hidden from all of us. We had all been living under a caste system that dehumanized everyone.

The Spanish caste system was adapted wherever Europeans colonized. Everyone who was under European rule became a party to Las Castas and the Doctrine of Discovery. As a result, they embodied the racial caste system they lived under, but each group internalized it differently. White-bodied people have internalized the racial caste, and it lives in them as supremacy, while Brown-bodied people have as colonization, limited freedom, opportunity, servitude, violation, betrayal, and displacement. Black bodies internalized the caste as enslavement, strife, danger, and lack of freedom.

SUPREMACY CONDITIONING AND PAYOFF

Supremacy allows for racial privilege. Privilege is access, immunity, innocence, goodness, freedom, and opportunity.

ACCESS

Whether White people are aware of it or not, they have access to opportunities People of Color can only dream of. From getting a mortgage to easier credit terms to a job, White people have invisible means of support that allow them to climb the ladder of success with greater ease than People of Color. That doesn't mean they don't have to work hard. It simply means they can get the job that allows them to work hard.

IMMUNITY

From the beginning of colonization, White people have been able to literally get away with murder. Take, for instance, lynchings. These public spectacles, well attended by White communities, saw more than three thousand Black men, women, and children murdered in public. While the bodies often hung on trees for hours or even days, White people were allowed to go home, get on with their lives, and no one was ever punished. It was the same with race riots. In January 2021, a White mob infiltrated the US Capitol looking to hang then vice president Mike Pence. They erected gallows on the Capitol grounds, broke into offices, stole computers and documents, and they were allowed to simply walk away, get on planes, and fly home.

INNOCENCE

For nearly one hundred years after the Emancipation Proclamation, White people could murder a Black person in public with no repercussion. They could steal Black people's property with no repercussion. Such was the case with my friend, Hay. The name was changed to protect his identity. When Hay was a little boy, he was visiting his grandfather in North Carolina. His grandparents had a washtub in their backyard. One day, a policeman drove by in a cruiser. He doubled back, got out of the car, went into his grandparents' backyard, and stole the washtub.

Hay, who was seven years old at the time, said to his grandfather, rather loudly, *"Aren't you going to do anything?!"* His grandfather covered Hay's mouth and pulled both of them away from the window. Hay said he was angry with his grandfather for not doing anything to recoup the washtub. It was in one of the healing racism seminars he got in touch with his rage. He was able to realize his grandfather was trying to save both of their lives that day. Hay was able to put his misplaced anger where it belonged—on the shoulders of the policeman who stole the tub. He was able to forgive his grandfather and see he stayed quiet out of love.

GOODNESS

White people pride themselves on being paragons of goodness and law-abiding citizens. Accusing them of being racists directly attacks their virtue. They believe racists are the "bad" people in society, and they are not like them. They don't understand racism is not about character; it's about conditioning.

FREEDOM

White people see themselves as entitled to freedom, even if they have to jail everyone else to get it. The problem with that is if you usurp another's freedom, you jail yourself by default. You will forever need to guard against their escape, and in the process, you, as the jailer, become the prisoner.

FEAR OF THE REVOLT

"*What if they do to us what we have done to them*" is one of those implicit beliefs behind a lot of the interactions we see between White people and People of Color. My West Indian grandmother used to always say, "*A thief judges by his own conditions*," meaning if you do others wrong, you will have no peace. You will live with the fear and expectation that someday they will do to you as you have done to them.

But if you refer to axiology, that fear is unfounded. Black and Brown people don't want to take from White people. They simply want the same opportunities for themselves. They don't want to be blocked in their progress. Sometimes young people say it best, as is the case of these two high school students highlighted below.

I was attending a high school presentation where students were engaged in a privilege exercise. It's an old exercise and has been done in workshops all over the US. I have been doing it in my seminars for years. It's called the "Walk of Privilege." In this exercise, the participants stand shoulder to shoulder in a line that stretches to either side of the room. The facilitator then reads a list of questions, and they are instructed to step forward, step back, or stay where they are depending on the statement. For example, the facilitator may say, *"If you are sure you can walk into any store in the US and find Band-Aids in your skin color, step forward." "If your parents went to college, step forward." "If your parents owned their own home, step forward. If not, step back."* And so on. At the end of the exercise, the participants are asked to look around and see where they ended up. They are then asked how they ended up there. No matter how many times I have done this exercise, the results are always the same: White males in front, followed by White women, Brown people in the middle, and Black people in the back.

OPPORTUNITY

White people have been conditioned to believe access and opportunity have always been equal to all. They believe those who don't succeed are at fault, not as smart, or somehow less than themselves. While on the surface, access and opportunity, also known as White privilege, are invisible to White people, it is one of the things that hurt White people. Racism is access, and opportunity is institutionalized, systemic, and interpersonal. An example of institutionalized White access and opportunity is the GI Bill, which gave low-interest loans to White soldiers returning from the Second World War while denying mortgages to Black and Brown soldiers who fought for their country and world peace in the same war.

An example of interpersonal access and opportunity is seen in the labor market. *"African-American college students are about as likely to get hired as Whites who have dropped out of high school,"* so says a new report from a non-profit called Young Invincibles. They analyzed data from the Bureau of Labor Statistics and the US Census. They examined the effect race and education levels have on unemployment. In the words of Rory O'Sullivan, deputy director of Young Invincibles:

"We were startled to see just how much more education young African-Americans must get in order to have the same chance at landing a job as their White peers."

According to an article in *Forbes* called "White High School Drop-Outs Are as Likely to Land Jobs as Black College Students" by Susan Adams, we forget people tend to hire for comfort, and those who are doing the hiring are often White people. White people often make hiring decisions based on whom they will feel more comfortable spending eight hours of their day with.

White people are often blind to the opportunities they have access to by the color of their skin. There seems to be little awareness that having the odds fixed in their favor infantilizes them. It's like having your parents do your math homework for you and not understanding why you failed the test. As a result of this access and opportunity, White people often suffer from imposter syndrome. Empower Work, a nonprofit organization, whose mission is to create healthy and equitable workplaces, describes it this way: *"Imposter syndrome is the feeling you haven't earned your success, you simply got lucky, and you're a fraud or "imposter" around people who actually earned it and know what they're doing."* You live in fear of others finding out how little you know about the job.

When the students finished the "Walk of Privilege" exercise, two boys, one White and one Black, best friends of the same socioeconomic background, were surprised to see they didn't end up next to each other. The White student said, *"I want my friend to have the same opportunities I have, but I don't want to give up my status."* The Black student said, "I don't want you to have to give up anything. I simply want the opportunity to acquire the same things." What the Black student didn't say was "the same things with the same amount of effort;" it was not having to work twice as hard to acquire the same things.

BROWN BODIES AND THE CASTE

Brown bodies have internalized the racial caste as colonization, and what was internalized depended on the country. But one thing all colonized countries have in common is the violence Europeans used to take over the land, the genocide that ensued, the misappropriation of property, and the impoverishment of the people. Colonization is *"the action or process of settling among and establishing control over the Indigenous people of an area. The action of appropriating a place or domain for one's own use,"* according to the Oxford English Dictionary.

Colonization often lives within the colonized as Stockholm syndrome, which is defined as over-identification and looking to be as much like their enslavers/kidnappers as possible. It also lives in the Brown community in the form of serving the colonizers. In many of the colonized countries, the Indigenous were forced to serve those who had colonized them, and if they didn't, it meant their lives. Their conditioning included:

ILLEGITIMACY

Your very existence is illegal. Marriage laws were set against them. Children born outside of marriage had no rights, and legal marriage was institutionalized for Europeans and the legal descendants born under a legal marriage. Europeans were not allowed to marry outside of their caste. Doing so would mean punishment and, in some cases, death.

SERVITUDE

Servitude is the state of being subject to those more powerful than yourself. It is a form of slavery. Your only job is to serve your master (el patron) and to serve as a stand between and a go-between.

LAND IN EXCHANGE FOR LIFE

The Indigenous who survived mass murder and disease had their land, possessions, women, and children taken away. They were at the whim of their rulers.

WRONG

Their ways are different from what their colonizers were used to, therefore they were wrong in their ways of dressing, worship, and even their ways of knowing, so they had to be converted.

LIMITED FREEDOM

Even to this day, Brown men and women are incarcerated at higher rates than White people. They are surpassed only by African-Americans.

BLACK BODIES AND THE CASTE

If you're a Black body, everything that applied to the Brown body applied to you and more. You internalize the racial caste system as colonization and enslavement. You were forced to work for no pay for perpetuity. Your body and soul belonged to the enslavers who could do with you as they pleased at any time, including killing you, and they would not be punished. Their conditioning was imposed and ingrained through centuries of violence. This includes being:

GUILTY

Black people are the scapegoats of society. They are blamed for what goes wrong and even for crimes that happened while they were absent from the crime scene. Black people are often seen as guilty and have to prove themselves innocent.

WRONG

From the time Europeans set foot on African soil, they saw people who dressed differently, sheltered differently, worshipped differently, and saw the world differently than themselves. This was seen as savage, unruly, and countered the "order" their cold climate dictated.

BAD

You are engrained in the belief there is something wrong with you and you are inherently not good, not as good as, or not good enough.

UNWORTHY OF OPPORTUNITY

You don't deserve anything worth having, including housing, education, money, or even medical care.

This is the premise of mass incarceration of Black citizens. Make no mistake about this; land restriction is not the only thing from the Doctrine of Discovery that is being used today. Under the papal bulls of the 1400s, you are to be enslaved for perpetuity and your possessions owned by the descendants, successors, and heirs, forever.

The upshot of all of this is we all internalized the institutionalized dysfunction created by centuries of racial conditioning, and so, we all need healing, regardless of the color of our skin. Worth mentioning again:

- Race is not real. Race is a myth.

- The myth of race is the conditioning we have all absorbed over hundreds of years.

- The racial conditioning we absorbed caused the condition we now call racism.

- The condition of racism is what we are looking to heal.

- We need to dismantle institutionalized and systemic conditioning.

Again, racism is a White problem. In a 2007 article in the *Harvard Gazette* entitled *Albert Einstein Civil Rights Activist*, Ken Gewertz writes of a little-known visit Albert Einstein made to Lincoln University in Pennsylvania in 1946. *"Einstein gave a speech in which he called racism "a disease of White people."* He added, *"I do not intend to be quiet about it."* Einstein also received an honorary degree and gave a lecture on relativity to Lincoln students. Lincoln University was the first university in the US to grant college degrees to African-Americans. Langston Hughes and Thurgood Marshall both attended Lincoln University.

While the inequalities set by the caste system affect all people and create disparities across the board, supremacy holds advantages that keep the system firmly in place. Supremacy gives White people choices People of Color do not have. The greatest among those is the power to choose. White people can choose when, where, and how they will interact with People of Color, if at all.

HERE ARE SOME QUESTIONS TO CONSIDER:

- What role is supremacy playing in your life?

- If you are a White person, are you aware of your supremacy status?

- How would equity affect you as a White person?

- If you are a Person of Color, how does racial supremacy play out in your life?

- As a Person of Color, how would equity affect you?

- What is the opportunity presented to the White community by seeing racism as White people's problem?

CHAPTER 15

THE THREE LANGUAGES OF THE CASTE

———

"A different language is a different vision of life."
—FEDERICO FELLINI

Communication is more than words. The language of the caste is not always expressed in words. The language of the caste is more often expressed in behavior, and when it comes to race, that behavior is tied to our racial conditioning. We are not looking at language from the perspective of linguistics or Ebonics, which is not a dialect, but a language in its own right spoken by African-Americans. What we are looking to do here is look at how the caste system impacts what we say and even think. As mentioned in the previous chapter, White people absorbed the system as supremacy, Brown people internalized the system as colonization, and Black people internalized the system as enslavement.

What does all of this have to do with interracial communication? Plenty! Consider this: How many times have you heard a White politician come to the defense of a White colleague who has been accused of saying or doing something racist? Has a Person of Color ever told you something you said or did was racist and you took it as an insult? Let's unpack that through the filters of the caste system.

For members of the White community, the caste system has created specific parameters through which you are judged and measured. Being White means you are:

- An upstanding citizen.

- A law-abiding citizen.

- A good person.

- A lovable person.

- Someone fair and just.

- Someone by whom the standard of beauty is measured.

- Someone whose looks and character are considered to be all goodness and purity. Moreover, you judge the rest of the world through those filters and make relationship decisions based on what you know of yourself and the world. We call it implicit bias.

Given the above list, when someone, White or a Person of Color, tells a White person their action or words are racist, what the White person hears is they are bad or wrong. To be more explicit, what is being pointed out is the White person is acting out of their unconscious, internalized racial conditioning. But they hear what is being said through the filters of supremacy's "White is right," and all of the good qualities that go along with that just became negated.

The stress response gets triggered, so now they want to fight (defend themselves and others), flee (they escape from the conversation), or go into paralysis (they don't know what to say).

Let's stop for a moment and consider we don't see your racial blind spots because we are conditioned not to see them. Still, those blind spots show up in the action, reactions, and interactions such as conversations. These interactions are recognized and received by People of Color as microaggressions and harm the listener. Often White people don't want to participate in the race conversation for precisely this reason; they fear saying the wrong thing. The problem is staying away from the conversation means nothing changes.

It is important to say here there are people who take great pleasure in calling people names. Calling someone a racist without an understanding of the conditioning that created it is sometimes a way to vent frustration, be vengeful, and perpetuate that dysfunctional behavior of name-calling that keeps us trapped.

If we are going to be serious about healing, transformation, and having conversations on race, we must first understand each group speaks from its place in the caste system. Each group in the caste system has created its own language. The members of that group speak from their understanding of the world. In the language of supremacy, the conversation stems from the list above.

The undercurrent that White people are supreme, that they are first in the hierarchy and are the most knowledgeable and powerful, keeps us from exploring different ways of being and knowing. While White people are very faithful to counting and measuring, they often dismiss other ways of knowing and using different senses. Indigenous knowledge is often intuitive.

For instance, my grandmother always knew when it was going to rain. As I allowed my intuition to become more acute, I was able to detect there is a fragrance the soil puts out just before it rains, even while it's sunny. But you can only smell it when you are close to nature. To detect that smell, you have to know what the air smells like when it is not raining. She knew that from experience, not from reading it in a book.

The patriarchal "father knows best" attitude and transactional relationships do not go down well in Communities of Color. The belief White people have the solution for everyone else and they should do as they do and say has been and continues to be problematic for people for whom the highest value is in the relationship. Supremacist-subordinate is often how White people handle domestic problems and foreign affairs. It's how they've handled race and racism for hundreds of years.

The problem with that thinking is it negates how the wealth was acquired in the first place. Forgotten has been the history of human toil, the exploitation of natural resources, and the violence used in its acquisition. It negates others' contributions, keeps us from having healthy relationships, and robs us of authentic communication.

White people defending other White people by saying their White friend is not a racist, they have never known that person to be racist, that makes perfect sense when you understand through their White filters, that person does not sound racist. Of course! They have never been racist to you, and you're both White. When a White person makes a racist remark, they don't sound racist to other White people because you both speak the same language and say similar things about Black people and People of Color. So, no, they don't sound racist to you if you're White. But to a person whose life could be endangered or who could lose their livelihood because of what a White person says that remark can have different implications. People of Color have learned to be careful listeners just to know if they are safe in an environment.

In Black communities, the language of the caste is more about how to stay safe and survive as one moves forward, and it looks to create a better life for self and family. Black people have an acute sensitivity to racist speech and a keen awareness of their surroundings. Survival is about knowing who you're safe with, so the racism gauge is acute and sensitive. Sometimes Black people act out of the conditioning without being aware of their implicit bias.

I was sitting in a restaurant with a Black woman friend. There was a White man seated across from us. The Black waitress, who had told us she was from Ethiopia, was in the middle of taking our order. The White man signaled to her, and in the middle of a sentence, she immediately went over to find out what he wanted. I couldn't believe it. My friend and I were surprised and appalled at her behavior. Needless to say, it became a teaching moment. We asked her why she didn't finish with us before going to him. She became defensive. All we did was ask a question, but my sense was somewhere within her, at that moment, the question hit her, and she felt what she had done. She then started to cry and went in the back to ask someone else to serve us. All we did was ask a simple question.

Then there are the actions, reactions, and interactions Black people have with each other that are squarely rooted in the caste system. There's the preoccupation with what other Black people do with their hair. Is it natural, straight, or purchased? There's skin color classification—how light or dark the person's skin tone may be. There's hearing someone was killed by the police and asking what the person did wrong. Was he running away? Why was the person running away, did he do something wrong? There's hearing something happened and hoping the person who did it was not Black. All these behaviors have their roots in the racial conditioning induced by the caste, and there are deeper roots that have social implications.

Trauma can bring on early puberty. During times of slavery, Black girls as young as nine years old would begin their menstrual cycle. Because every enslaved human was worth money, the slave owners were looking to grow a large "crop" of slaves. Girls as young as ten years old were being raped by their owners, friends, and family members. Moreover, the enslaved boys were forced to mate with the girls, again, to produce more slaves for the system. The children were the property of the slave owner, who could rent or sell these children as young as three years old to work in the fields of their friends and neighbors. The boys who fathered these children had no say in their lives, and the children took the last name of their owner. The mothers of these young Black girls had to prepare their daughters to submit in order to spare their lives. No one could complain. The best one could do was run away.

Running brought on a different kind of danger, not just to the ones running, but to those left behind. Policing your neighbor and making sure no one ran away was the responsibility of the enslaved, so keeping secrets was important, individually and as groups. The language of the runaway slaves was written in the hymns and sung on the fields. "Wade in the Water" is one of those songs with a message for runaway slaves. One of the ways to throw off the dogs following the scent of the runaway was to hide in or cross water. Another example of messages in songs is "Follow the Drinking Gourd," which refers to the constellations known as the Big Dipper and the Little Dipper. This song was used by conductors of the underground railroad.

"Where the great big river meets the little river
Follow the drinking gourd.
For the old man is a-waiting to carry you to freedom
If you follow the drinking gourd."

Black and Brown families have to teach their children to stay safe in a racially charged environment while trying not to traumatize them into paralysis. When to have the safety conversation is another issue. We don't want to scare the child into hopelessness, and we want to maintain their innocence, but how? Don't put your hands in your pocket while in a store. Put your hands on the wheel of the car when stopped by the police and don't make any sudden moves. Even if you follow the law to the letter, you may still not make it home. With all that's coming at you, you also have to speak softly, don't express anger, especially at work. The language of the caste for Black people is to express yourself when you're with your own, but know in a White environment, that same expression could cause you problems. Your language of safety is "be non-threatening to Whites," which often means "don't be yourself."

Brown communities range from hypersensitivity to ove-ridentification with White people. Many are preoccupied with lightening their skin and the texture of their hair. They want nothing to do with anything that identifies them as Black. There is a discomfort with White people and an inherent distrust, but their allegiance is made clear by their behavior. They often struggle with belonging outside of their communities. Having been trained by the same caste system like everyone else and feeling like they don't belong with White people or Black people, per se, they stay close to their own communities, at times refusing to learn the language for fear of losing their identity and/or anger at the system.

While we continue to communicate without the awareness we are shouting through our internalized, racially conditioned filters, we will continue to trip over each other, thinking we are right and everyone else is wrong. Meanwhile, all we are doing is speaking the language of the caste, the language of segregation, and segregated people are easier to control and thereby condition.

We can become better communicators if we understand while we have all lived under the same caste system, we have all internalized that system based on the place our society has assigned us. Whether we are aware of it or not, we communicate out of what we have internalized. Healing leads us to have more authentic communications, regardless of where we live in the caste system.

Now you have some context and awareness of how racism was institutionalized, as well as the systems that continually support it. This lets you see how we have all been racialized and the ways our racial conditioning affects us. We can now begin the process of healing.

In Part Two of this book, we will look at how we heal. In the meantime, to enhance interracial communication in the era of Black Lives Matter, we need to:

- Become race literate.

- Increase our understanding of the language of our part of the caste.

- Be humble in our expression.

- Ask more questions.

- Listen with an open mind and an open heart.

PART 2

THE STAGES OF THE HEALER'S CODE

CHAPTER 16

INTRODUCTION TO THE STAGES OF THE HEALER'S CODE

"*We learn and heal in ebbs and flows, spiraling around the center of ourselves where our true Self dwells. When we're in a cycle of growth, we burn through layers of ego fears and touch into that core place of wellness where peace and clarity reside. Our hearts are open and alive, and we can receive and give love with ease. This is the gold of being human, and how we long to live there always! But alas, inevitably, when the false self senses we're growing 'too much' or learning 'too quickly,' it bucks like a bull at a bronco, and it suddenly feels like we're back at square one. Then we cycle into the ebb stage, and if we don't have a context in which to understand the cycle of healing, the fear-mind can easily grab hold of these ebbs as evidence to support our current anxiety story.*"

—SHERYL PAUL, "THE CYCLE OF HEALING"

I knew I needed to be healed. I looked for counseling, but the counselors available to me at that time in my life didn't know what I knew about racism. They didn't see what I saw. Life was different for them, and I knew that. It was the 1980s, and the counselors available to me in Washington state in the US were White young women who had no clue of what I was speaking. I knew I needed healing and had nowhere to turn. If it was to be, it was up to me. I looked for help and sought teachers, but none were available to me at the time. By the 1990s, I turned to the one source that might be of help—books. I read everything I could get my hands on, but the books I felt drawn to were about spirituality, and I can't explain why. It just felt like I was not going to find the solace I needed in academic works unless I needed to research history or experiments. Books became my teachers, counselors, and friends. I was especially interested in the intersection of science and spirituality. I read books by Emmet Fox, Annalee Skarin, and Catherine Ponder. Later, I read books by Deepak Chopra, Gregg Braden, and Caroline Myss. I read and eventually became a teacher of *A Course in Miracles*. I studied Reiki, Magnified Healing, and the healing power contained in our mind and body.

Through this process, my intuition was sharpened, and I learned about the healing power of the human voice. I had trained to become an opera singer in my teen years, and now I had a new use for that training. I became a sound therapist and taught others to use their voice as a healing tool. All the while, I was becoming emotionally stronger, more self-empowered, and more grounded. During this time, my life fell apart more than once, but I just kept going. I became divorced with three children and received no child support. The divorce left us homeless.

We temporarily stayed with family or friends. I had one full-time and two part-time jobs and went back to school for a second degree. It was almost as if I had a destination, although I wasn't sure where it was headed. I continued to study. Eventually, the pieces of the puzzle started to come together and fall into place.

I started teaching others what I was learning, sharing with them the history that was not being taught in schools, and I began to see myself and my ancestors differently. I began to see my wholeness. I learned there is something in us humans beyond resilience. There is something powerful in us that is untouched by the trauma, the pain, and the fear. It is that place in us where resilience comes from, and that inner place became my teacher.

In all the years I have devoted to the healing process, I rarely, if ever, heard anyone speak about race and racism as something that needed to be healed. Racism was always about something that needed to change or something we needed to learn about, but we would not dig deeper. Healing is both powerful and delicate. Yes, healing from racism requires knowledge, and we absolutely need to change and make changes in the outer world; healing from racism requires a deeper dive. And while one seeks to inflict no harm, we know healing is going to hurt. It's like setting a broken leg. If you leave it the way it is, you may never be able to walk the same way again. Resetting it is painful, but you know the pain is a necessary part of the healing needed for the transformation to happen.

This book is about the healing of racism. To be more precise, it is about healing the racial conditioning we have internalized over centuries. I am writing this book in the middle of what is being called a global pandemic, COVID-19.

Lockdown is not easy. Many may feel claustrophobic from being with family members twenty-four seven. Others may feel alone and scared. Loss of freedom can bring up feelings of grief, anger, and overwhelm. Loss of freedom is exactly what Black people and People of Color live with from the moment they are born until they die. The stages of healing I write about in this book are a combination of the Kübler-Ross model, Dr. Fr. Clarence Williams' work in racial sobriety, and my own process. May this model give you information that justifies how you may be feeling, and may it offer you hope, as there are several stages before and after the Kübler-Ross model I added to complete the prescription. Healing from racism required these extra steps.

AWAKENING

Stage 1: Innocence–In this stage, you're going about your life as normal. You believe the whole world to be as the world is for you.

Stage 2: Ignorance–We ignore what is before our very eyes.

GRIEVING

Stage 3: Denial–Something happens to jolt you into attention. It's unpleasant, and you don't want to deal with it. You want to go back to sleep and not be disturbed with this stuff, so you go into denial. Denial maintains dysfunction; you deny what is happening, pretend it's not real, not yours, and it's out there in other people. You defend your position and get angry when people bring up the subject.

Stage 4: Anger–This stage can be implosive (hurting the self, overindulging, abusing substances, overeating, drinking).

Anger can also be explosive, lashing out, being verbally, physically, or emotionally abusive.

Stage 5: Bargaining–In this stage, we try negotiating with the circumstances. If I do X, I may be able to change things, or at least make them better. When we do all that, we can find the circumstances don't change, or they continue to be beyond our control, and we get depressed.

Stage 6: Depression–This is the "never going to" stage. It's never going to change or get better. I don't have any control here. Nothing I do makes an impact. I feel hopeless and helpless.

HEALING

Stage 7: Acceptance–Here we are accepting the circumstances as they are. This stage allows us to think differently and get creative, and that's when we reengage.

Stage 8: Reengage–In this stage, we engage with the world, the circumstances, and the people involved from a new perspective. You've been through an experience that has left you wiser, bitter, enlightened, or scarred. No matter what, you are forever changed. *"No man steps into the same river twice, for it is not the same river, and he is not the same man."* —Heraclites

Stage 9: Forgiveness–This is a choice where we release without blame. It is available to you for your peace of mind, open heart, and an unencumbered path forward. Forgiveness of self and others releases us to be a powerful witness.

BECOMING EMPOWERED

Stage 10: Witnessing–This is more than just the telling of the story. Witnessing is also about how we show up. It's about how you use the wisdom garnered through the process to make life better for yourself and others.

Stage 11: Processing–Taking the time to breathe and examine. Take note of where you've been and where you are. Notice new feelings and sensations. Do you see things differently because you have had an experience?

Stage 12: Vision–What kind of a world do you want to see? Create a vision and begin to move toward it.

Stage 13: Taking Action–In this stage, we take action from a place of inner wholeness. We have a sense of knowing our place in the world. Our service is empowered from within. There is a confidence that there is something we can do to make a difference. When we do something about our situation, we feel greater sovereignty over our lives.

These are the stages of healing. Each stage is explained in greater detail in the chapters to follow. As you read, notice the places where you get stuck when it comes to racism. Don't make this session about "those people" out there; make it about you. Feel the feelings and the emotions that come up for you. Feel the places you carry anger in your body, or where you carry grief or joy and peace, and remember to *breathe*!

QUESTIONS TO CONSIDER:

- How do you know when you're healing?

- Do these stages resonate with you?

- What makes you feel whole?

CHAPTER 17

HOW WE CAN HEAL

WHAT NEEDS TO CHANGE?
WHO NEEDS TO CHANGE?

"They always say time changes things, but you actually have to change them yourself."

—ANDY WARHOL

When we speak about race and racism, we are talking about nearly six hundred years of misinformation, violence, theft, lies, colonization, forced labor camps, kidnapping, enslavement, bad science, ignorance, generations of trauma, and continued oppression. Racism has revealed and continues to reveal the worst of humanity. How can we heal from all of that? And who needs to heal?

As mentioned earlier in this book, when it comes to racism, we all need healing. But the problem is in a society where the highest value is placed on what one can count and measure, as mentioned in the chapter "Race, Latitude, & Attitude," we want to transform racism by quantifying it. We've been doing that for decades. We have tons of research information about racial disparities, inequalities, violence, abuse, and microaggressions. We know a lot about what is wrong. Transforming racism in organizations and in schools has become an intellectual exercise, a kind of "what/who you know" in the anti-racism world. Whom have you read? Who are your heroes and heroines? But in spite of all we have learned and all the knowledge we now have, as the kids would say, *"How's that working for you?"* The healing of racism is not just about changing minds; it's about changing hearts. Racism is emotional for most people. Healing is about looking within, being conscious of our fears and triggers, and taking responsibility for our actions, reactions, and interactions. We already know we can change laws, and that helps, but if people don't change, they will continue to act out of their internalized racial conditioning. They will create laws that continually adhere to the caste system and harm People of Color. Despite all the civil rights laws we have in place, we still see people through the filters of our racial conditioning.

Emotions are the entryway into the heart. Teaching people not to feel or to ignore feelings when they come up detaches them from their humanity. Our feelings interact with our senses, our organs, and our hormones, creating a reaction in our hearts that shows up in our electromagnetic field, our human energy field. That field introduces us to the world before our bodies even get there, as the heart's electromagnetic field extends beyond the human body. According to the HeartMath Institute's book *Science of the Heart - Exploring the Role of the Heart in Human Performance*, we learn:

> *The heart's electrical field is about sixty times greater in amplitude than the electrical activity generated by the brain. This field, measured in the form of an*

electrocardiogram (ECG), can be detected anywhere
on the surface of the body. Furthermore, the magnetic
field produced by the heart is more than one hundred
times greater in strength than the field generated by
the brain and can be detected up to three feet away
from the body, in all directions, using SQUID-based
magnetometers. Moreover, the field produced by the
heart affects the people around us.

The Oxford English Dictionary describes resilience as
"the capacity to recover quickly from difficulties." There are
some very inconvenient truths in this book, including some
which may make you uncomfortable. Some may make you
angry and some may make you cry. But you are resilient. You
can bounce back stronger and more empowered than ever
because this time, your healing will not be based on a myth.
The way most of us learned history was as if we can't handle
the truth, but we can. We are strong, powerful, and resilient.
More than anything, we deserve to know the truth.

When it comes to race and racism, People of Color are
amazingly resilient. Resilience is meant to be used to bounce
back from difficult or traumatic situations. In fact, no one
knows how resilient they are until they've been tried in the
burning coals of life. But to be tried daily, weekly, monthly
for centuries and still access resilience is a testimony to the
power Black and Brown people possess.

Healing is not an academic exercise. Healing is about
engaging all the parts of the self—mind, body, spirit, and
emotions—to create new ways of being. Healing is about
becoming greater than the pain, gaining a new way of seeing
self and others, and creating new connections with the world
and its people. Healing racism is about coming home to the

human family. Healing is about connecting the past to the present to understand the present and using that understanding to create a better tomorrow.

There are four parts to the Healer's Code: *awakening*, *grieving*, *healing*, and *wholeness*. We have looked at history, trauma, what healing is, and who needs healing. In the following chapters, we will look at the Healer's Code and how to apply it to heal from our racial conditioning. We will walk through the stages of the Healer's Code, also known as the stages of healing.

In the end, healing is a choice to find inner peace and grounding despite the toxicity. It is about tapping into our reservoirs of inner compassion for self and the world. Healing is about using your resilience to become a peaceful warrior. Healing is about choosing self-love.

Remember you can't heal or change others. The best you can do is share your learning and process and serve as a living example. What they do with that information is beyond your control. Focus on your own healing and look for ways to make a difference in the world. It is the best use of your energy and time. This is a problem that affects the entire human family. Every person in the global village is needed.

**AS WE GO INTO HEALING,
HERE ARE SOME QUESTIONS TO CONSIDER:**

- Do you believe you need healing from racism? If so, why do you believe that?

- Are there people in your life in need of racial healing?

- What do you hope to get out of this process?

CHAPTER 18

WHAT IS THE HEALER'S CODE?

HOW I CAME TO THE HEALER'S CODE

"That's not our disease. Keep working."

—ELZEIRA ROBBINS

In the space of thirty-plus years of my own healing journey and assisting a few thousand people of different backgrounds, I learned some things that became invaluable to me. That learning became the foundation of the Race Healer's Code. The Healer's Code itself has thirteen stages, and each stage is explained in the next chapter. But for now, these are the guiding principles that led to the Healer's Code, specifically the "Race Healer's" Code.

The idea of race was created by those in power to justify keeping people in bondage, extract free labor, control the economy and the narrative, and build wealth for themselves and their families. Racism, the idea certain groups are superior to others based on their physical characteristics, is the result of hundreds of years of conditioning facilitated by the myth of race. Race is not real, but racism is! Healing such a deep wound, as well as the normalized dysfunction it supports, will take time.

Racism is institutional, systemic, internalized, personal, and interpersonal. For hundreds of years, the myth of race has controlled the narrative. We can heal from racism, but to do so, we must understand what we are really dealing with. We institutionalize something by turning it into law. We then set up systems to support what is institutionalized. This includes neighbor-to-neighbor policing. People born under these systems internalize what is institutionalized, accepting it as "just the way things are," and act out of what is in their environment. Because the original history is hidden, there is no conscious context for the behavior. We call this unconscious bias. People internalize what they experience and act, react, and interact out of what has been learned, which they now believe to be normal. The dysfunction becomes normalized, and then people interact with each other out of what they have internalized.

We are *one human family*, and we all need healing from racism. No amount of racial conditioning can change the reality that we are one human family with all functions and dysfunctions we find in individual families. When it comes to healing from racism, we are each responsible for our own transformation. No one can heal for you, nor can you afford to wait for others to change to improve your life. You are worthy of healing now. Healing is the path to wholeness, something racism takes away from all of us.

You are a whole human—mind, body, spirit, and emotions—which means you will need to heal your racial conditioning at all levels. You deserve to claim your wholeness not tomorrow, not someday, but you are worthy of your wholeness now! The great news is no matter what has happened in your life, your wholeness is still intact, waiting for you to remove what keeps you from experiencing it. Your wholeness holds the truth of who you are—your gifts, your power, your beauty, your grace, and in spite of it all, your innocence.

Innocence cannot be an excuse for ignorance. Awareness is a powerful healer. If we are going to be serious about healing our racial divide, race literacy will have to be at the forefront of the process. Awareness gives you information to transform your life, and that information gives you a choice; choice is a superpower.

We often take our ability to choose for granted. Choice is inextricably linked to free will, and free will is a divine right. You cannot heal what you have no awareness of, but you can choose to become aware.

If we can't own our shadow, our shadow will own us. Healing requires we accept the truth of what has been. It requires we acknowledge and accept our share of the dysfunction, change our ways, and make things right. If we are going to heal from racism, we have to accept the shadow side of our history and look to make amends. Shadow work, which is looking at the violent, unloving, fear-based side of our nature, is essential to the healing process.

Intergenerational and historical race trauma are silent stressors, and therefore silent killers. People being shot, beaten, and killed are the most extreme ways racism claims lives. But there are other, subtler ways racism takes people's lives. The human body makes a chemistry for everything. Our subconscious stores every event in our lives and holds it like a silent treasure with the intent of keeping us safe. It stores every physical, emotional, mental, and spiritual experience we have ever had, and it holds our traumas. Research has shown trauma gets passed on from generation to generation as we saw in the work of Dr. Rachel Yehuda and the mice experiment mentioned previously in this book. We fall victim to known and unknown trauma until we become aware and decide to heal.

Racism is a problem *for* People of Color, not the problem *of* People of Color. Discernment is essential to the healing process. Whose pattern of behavior are you acting out of? Your family's? Your society's? How have you been conditioned to behave by our racialized system? Discernment can be the doorway to freedom and transformation. It can help you get clear, and clarity enables you to see what is yours to heal and what belongs to other people. Know racism is a problem *for* People of Color. Racism is not the problem *of* People of Color; therefore, People of Color cannot solve it. White people have to address racism. People of Color and Black people have to heal the many ways they have internalized the oppression and the survival patterns that have kept us alive and allowed us to thrive against all odds. Some of those patterns may not be serving us now.

You are only responsible for healing your share of the dysfunction. Let others do their own work. You can be compassionate and generous and share what you have learned if you wish. You can be an ally and walk side by side with others on the same journey of healing; this is very important. However, when it comes to racism in America, White people need to heal their racism (prejudice plus power), xenophobia, and internalized supremacy. And People of Color need to treat their internalized oppression, colorism, and Stockholm syndrome.

Anger is a natural part of the healing process. Anger is not to be feared, but to be embraced compassionately and with patience. Your anger does not define you. It is a feeling tied to an emotion whose very root is fear. Anger is what shows up when we feel lied to, deceived, abused, and betrayed. The anger will pass as you engage in healing. How you end up on the other side of that anger depends on the choices you make.

Learn as much as you can about the past. Your past is tied to your liberation. What you know or don't know about the past is affecting your worldview. If you want to change the future, find out how the past is affecting your present. Remember the words of George Santayana, *"Those who do not know history's mistakes are doomed to repeat them."*

What others say and do says a lot about them, not about you. What others say and do is about them, not about you. People can only see as far as their filters. The broader their worldview, the more accepting and gracious they tend to be.

Align yourself with peaceful, loving, joyous, and generous people. Better yet, become that yourself. You are in a position to be sovereign over your life and be the change you want to see in the world. You will become more effective if you choose to keep an open heart. It's not easy to stay open in the face of so much toxicity, but it is vital to your health and wealth.

Keep your heart open. There are times when it is hard to get out of our own way or deal with our pain. A loving smile opens the heart, and so do kind thoughts. An open heart opens the doors to the world.

Keep these principles in mind as you move through the Healer's Code, also known as the stages of healing. As you move through the process, you may discover where you have been unconscious, self-conscious, conscious, hyperconscious, or hyperaware regarding your reaction to race-related circumstances. You will also see your triggers.

Regardless of where you are in the healing process, the Healer's Code will assist you, as it has many others in healing relationships with self and others. You'll find a sense of rightness within yourself, a natural connection to the world, and a sense of wholeness. The Healer's Code outlined in this book is universal and can be applied to various areas of life, from personal to business. The Healer's Code will give you an understanding of what it takes to heal.

An often left-out piece of information in healing is the healing crisis. This is where things get worse before they get better. That's the time to be patient, compassionate, and engage in self-care. The next chapter is the doorway into the stages of healing: the Healer's Code.

To crack the Healer's Code, stay present and allow yourself to feel!

How it works:

In my two-day Race Demystified immersive experience (the foundation for this book), participants have found that it may take as long as forty-five days for the information to move through your system and become part of you. That means the learning becomes internalized, and you start to see yourself differently in relation to race. You can use the code to transform your life, organization, and community.

When you find parts that are particularly difficult, stop, breathe, feel, and process.

QUESTIONS TO CONSIDER:

- Does your racial conditioning serve you? If so, how does racial conditioning serve you?

- Are you willing to leave behind your racial conditioning?

- Can you imagine yourself free from racial conditioning? What might that feel like in your body?

AWAKENING

"Awareness is the first step in healing."
—DEAN ORNISH

CHAPTER 19

STAGES 1 & 2
INNOCENCE & IGNORANCE

———

**SOMEWHERE BETWEEN
INNOCENCE AND IGNORANCE
LIES YOUR AWAKENING**

People don't know what they don't know. But learning is required for a new consciousness to develop. In a world full of information, innocence cannot be used as an excuse for ignorance. Innocence refers to one's lack of guile and malice. Innocence is a state of purity in which one is uncorrupted or unaware of having been corrupted. Ignorance, however, carries with it a kind of awareness, as it is about something we are ignoring. The information is available, but we may not be aware the information is available. There is another form of ignorance; it is what we call willful ignorance. Willful ignorance is a choice. It is when the information is available, we know it is available, and we choose not to open ourselves to it. Willful ignorance is a conscious choice to remain asleep.

Black people and People of Color have never been asleep at the wheel of racism; they could not afford to be. Their very lives have been at stake. White people, however, live in a comparatively different world, and many have trouble understanding the experiences of people who are not White.

To be White means you don't have to think about race or racism as something that applies to you. A White person's conditioning means you decide when, where, and on what terms you will interact with People of Color. Being White means you don't have to think about how your skin color will impact your world on a daily basis. It means if you commit a crime, you will be seen as innocent and have to be proven guilty, as opposed to being seen as guilty and then having to prove your innocence. In situations where there is an absence of proof of guilt, a Black person's character is attacked ad nauseam.

Black children and Children of Color are born into a racial caste system that leaves very little room for their innocence and is set against them from the beginning. The loss of innocence happens early, and the continual stereotyping, racial stress, and racial trauma are relentless, causing life-course stress that may well be related to stress-related illnesses in their adult lives.

So what is innocence, and how does one lose it when it comes to race? According to *Merriam-Webster Dictionary*, innocence is "*freedom from legal guilt of a particular crime or offense, freedom from guilt or sin through being unacquainted with evil; blameless, lack of knowledge; ignorance; freedom from guile or cunning;*" and "*simplicity, lack of worldly experience or sophistication.*"

When it comes to racism, Children of Color lose their innocence early. The majority of kindergarten teachers in the US are White women who have been raised in unconscious or conscious supremacy. They sometimes carry an implicit fear of Black children, especially Black male children. Their implicit biases are seen in the numbers.

Black students in the United States are subject to disciplinary action at rates much higher than their White counterparts. These disciplinary actions put students at higher risk for negative life outcomes, including involvement in the criminal justice system.

This study conducted by Travis Riddle and Stacey Sinclair uses federal data and covers *"thirty-two million students at nearly ninety-six thousand schools"* in their research of *"racial disparities in school-based disciplinary actions are associate with county-level rates of racial bias."* This research has been done many times over with the same results. In several schools, the police have been called on Black children as young as five years old—not the parent, mental health officials, or someone who could lend aid to the child, but the police.

The loss to our children, especially Black children and Children of Color, is tremendous, and it involves the whole school. Children get labeled by other children as bad, something they had already picked up from living in a racialized system. The parents are traumatized. Many of these children live with fear the police are coming to get them, and they are triggered every time they see a blue uniform. Because the teacher/school biases have been exposed, Parents of Color label the teacher and school racist and are now on guard. No matter which way you spin it, racism hurts everyone. If there was any innocence, everyone there has lost it.

Ignorance of the ways our collective racial conditioning affects White people is detrimental to Communities of Color. From educators to corporate managers, an education that is deeper than bias training is needed. While it is true we all have biases, racial biases are very distinct. Racial biases are institutional and systemic, absorbed through the culture and acted out in interpersonal relationships, such as a student-teacher relationship or a manager-employee relationship.

While innocence is not an excuse for ignorance, the way to tackle both is through race literacy. To heal racial ignorance, one has to become historically knowledgeable and self-aware. One has to become humble enough to admit ignorance and care enough to move out of willful ignorance. Most educators I know went into the field because they care about children. But their unconscious racial biases and conditioned racial fears can get in the way of their success as an educator. Even their expectations of their students are colored by their racial conditioning.

Healing is about awakening and becoming aware of the reality that when it comes to race and racism, we have all been badly trained. Awakening to our collective racial conditioning and the need to stay racially sober is essential to the process of transformation. We have to be open to learning from one another, be honest about the ways racism hurts our human family, and be willing to stay awake to how we add to the dysfunction.

As mentioned several times in this book, human beings are wired for connection. As a species, we would not have survived were it not for our dependency on each other. Parents, grandparents, siblings, and villagers all cared for the young. We descended from nomadic tribes traveling together, foraging for food, and hunting in groups to carry larger animals to feed the entire village. Human babies come into the world still connected to the mother through the umbilical cord. In our hearts, we long to connect with other humans. Segregation is not natural to our humanity. Healing takes a village.

Even while we flounder around in ignorance, our loss of innocence causes grief. We enter the doors of our grief denying racism is real or believing racism hurts some and not all. But there is no escaping the culture we live in, a racialized culture that, by its very nature, forces us to separate our heads from our hearts. It teaches us to give credence to our heads while denying the promptings of our hearts. So, we find ways to survive, and one of those ways is denial.

Somewhere in our innocence and ignorance, something happens to wake us up.

In the next two chapters, we will look at denial from generic to racial. Denial is where most of us enter the stages of grief. What are we grieving? The loss of our connections and thereby the loss of our humanity.

QUESTIONS TO CONSIDER:

- When and how did you lose your racial innocence?

- Have you ever hidden behind racial ignorance?

- As you consider the previous questions, how do you feel in your body?

- *Breathe!*

GRIEVING

"Grief is itself a medicine."
—WILLIAM COWPER

CHAPTER 20

GRIEVING & HEALING

———

"Grit your teeth and let it hurt. Don't deny it, don't be overwhelmed by it. It will not last forever."

—RABBI HAROLD KUSHNER

In order to heal, something must be sacrificed. We sacrifice our racial conditioning on the altar of wholeness. Healing our racial conditioning is about leaving behind the racialized self to reach our individual and collective wholeness. While racism may be unhealthy and dysfunctional, it's all we have known up to this point. It is familiar. So, we grieve. We grieve our loss of innocence. We grieve what was familiar. We grieve the loss of who we have been up to this point. We long for the days when we didn't know what we now know.

In the process of transformation, we will grieve over and over again. We grieve when we feel a sense of loss, and loss is what we feel when we discover the world we knew is not based on facts. We will grieve the loss of life, of wealth, of faith, and of trust in our systems. But if we allow ourselves to be vulnerable and feel the emotions, what we encounter on the other side is the truth of our humanity, resilience, and power. Who we are without the burden of our racial conditioning is nothing short of extraordinary! To get there, we will need to walk through the shadow, and we are brave enough and strong enough to do that. Put quite simply, we are enough!

As we awaken from our ignorance and our collective sleep to the truth of our lives and the various forms of segregation we face, grieving is an important part of healing and is what follows when we decide to let go of the past.

When we pop out of our ignorance and innocence, we can find ourselves lost and confused. We want to get our lives "back to normal" as soon as possible. But what we call normal is the past, where the self we are leaving behind lives, and we are not there anymore. Once we awaken, our lives are never the same again. If we are ever to heal from the past, we need to be honest with our process and allow time for grieving. We would do well to recognize we are not only grieving as individuals, but we are also doing collective grieving. We find ourselves grieving as a community, as a nation, and as a world. We grieve for our ancestors and all they went through. We grieve for nations and leaders. But most of all, we grieve for ourselves, for lost time and lost friendships, and for the self we thought we were. In many ways, our collective grieving and healing from racism is an acknowledgment of our oneness. We are all in this together.

We know we are grieving the obvious, the past that never was, the lost opportunities, the lost dreams, the belief in things that were not real, and the facts that were kept hidden from us. Along with all of this, we also grieve things that are not so obvious such as the loss of our innocence, of a sense of safety, and of our view of the world.

As a result of this grieving, feelings of powerlessness and sadness may at times be present. Tears and anger may surface seemingly out of nowhere. The work we do to support ourselves and our families takes second place to our emotions and may even feel pointless at times.

This is all part of the grieving process, and grieving is a natural part of healing. Conscious grieving—that is, consciously acknowledging our loss—will help us be present with what we are feeling in the moment and allow our hearts to begin the process of healing.

Trying to force ourselves into a "business as usual" mode may be unrealistic right now. This is a time to focus on what we are feeling in our hearts. A time to give ourselves grace and time. A wounded heart needs attention, it needs compassion, it needs love, but most of all, it needs time so we can strengthen ourselves into much-needed action.

Here are some things we can do in the moment...

When intense emotions surface, take time to *breathe*. Let yourself become aware of your breath. Take long, slow, deep breaths. Develop a breath count (counting slowly to five as you inhale and counting to five as you exhale). While taking long, deep breaths, imagine the air is coming directly into your chest instead of your nose and mouth. This will take your focus out of your head and bring it into the body, where you can easily access a greater sense of peace.

Speak about feelings and emotions. It's not always easy to speak about feelings, but expression is an important part of healing. Find someone you can trust to speak to about your feelings and emotions. Let the tears surface, even if you have to excuse yourself from a meeting and find a quiet place to cry.

Find where emotions are stored in your body. See if you can pinpoint the area of the body where you feel the anger, pain, sadness, or frustration. For a lot of people, it may be the stomach, chest, or neck. Inhale and exhale into that area of the body where you are feeling the emotions. Imagine the word 'peace' and breathe peace into that area of the body.

Be aware of your fears. The fear or pain you may be feeling as a result of your awakening may be causing personal, unconscious fears within your life to surface. When this happens, a situation that might have been easily solved may seem monumental. Ask yourself if what you are feeling or the way you are behaving is rational given the moment's circumstance.

Speak of what you are experiencing with family members or friends. Even very young children may be aware something is not quite right. Let your family know you are moving through some emotional times. It has nothing to do with them. They may benefit from knowing that.

As a final note, practice patience and compassion with yourself and others. Become a peaceful, unifying presence in your place of work and community. Share a word of comfort with another. There is enough fear out there; determine to be a light while you move through your own process and be patient with yourself when you can't.

When emotions are strong, one may need to be still and quiet rather than trying to have a conversation about anything, let alone race. Instead, give yourself time. Time has a way of putting things into perspective. Take time to collect your thoughts and ideas before attempting a conversation. Honor your feelings and emotions, but don't let them overtake you.

Time can give you the opportunity to speak from your heart instead of your anger.

As I began uncovering the history of race and racism, the grief I felt was overwhelming! I felt anger, rage, and great sorrow for myself, my family members, and my ancestors. I felt robbed and violated! I felt like part of my life had been stolen from me, like I had lost years of my life. And in some ways, I had. When I first learned about the Doctrine of Discovery, I took to my bed that weekend. I was devastated as I discovered I had indeed been robbed and violated, as had my ancestors. The grief was powerful! I cried, I raged, and for days, my anger was palpable. I couldn't stop talking about it. There again was a loss of innocence.

I knew Columbus' trip had changed the world, but I had no idea what hurled him into his journey was a papal doctrine that enslaved people like me. I had no idea the Doctrine of Discovery was still being used today to settle cases in the Supreme Court in the US, as well as courts in Canada and Australia. I didn't know it was institutionalized globally. Beyond the Doctrine of Discovery being used to deny Indigenous peoples' land rights, I began to connect the implications of a law that was to enslave non-Christians for perpetuity. The way the doctrine reads, it's as if it is connected to the incarceration rates, to Black and Brown men and women being killed on the streets by police, to how Whites over time have killed Blacks and People of Color in public and have never been punished for their crime. The Doctrine of Discovery felt strangely connected to disparities in housing, banking, salaries, and so on. It literally made me sick!

Grieving is an important part of the healing process. We don't want to skip over our grief. Grieving is important to racial healing. We don't want to skip over the gifts that grief can give us, gifts such as deeper compassion and greater awareness.

Expect that grief will come up, and I say come up because the grief is already there. What you learn as you discover the truth brings it to the surface. To heal from racism, we have to be willing to give up our racialized ways to live in the oneness of the human family.

QUESTIONS TO CONSIDER:

- As you start healing, what part of your racial conditioning will you miss?

- What will you miss being right about?

- Who in your circle of influence will be most uncomfortable with your change?

- Did you ever think you would be grieving the loss of racism?

As you will encounter in the next chapter, denial is the first stage of the grieving process.

CHAPTER 21

STAGE 3
DENIAL

———

"Denial is the suture that keeps the dagger in place. A people in denial can't change anything because, in denial, there is nothing that needs to change. To make the changes necessary, we must take an honest look at where we are and how we got here."

—MILAGROS PHILLIPS

Many of us enter the stages of healing from our racial conditioning by being awakened from our denial. Something or someone helps us to recognize there is something we have failed to see, to recognize, or to acknowledge. If we dare to look beyond that which is familiar to us, there is a glorious door that opens and invites us to walk through the experience of a different world. This world presents us with opportunities to look at what we chose not to look upon before and accept the gift we passed by—the gift of healing.

Taking those initial steps through that door into this unfamiliar world takes courage. We know beyond those gates, we can no longer face the world as separate from ourselves, and through the doors of racial healing, we become one with the world. Through those doors is the tunnel of the shadows we denied and even the world we all conspired to maintain. But if we allow ourselves the fullness of the journey, we come through to the other side with new wisdom, knowledge, and perhaps even the courage to lead others across the bridge to recovery.

The problem is when we are hardwired in our denial, we cannot make the changes that can lead to new experiences. Denial keeps us from seeing how our actions and decisions may be hurting others, and it can keep us stuck. Sometimes we hang on to our denial because of pride or for historical reasons. Sometimes we fail to see it's not just our history that has to be considered, but also how the past and traditions we may consider to be great may be hurting others.

I had been invited to speak to a school system in the Midwest. They were looking at the name of the high school football team and their mascot. The name of the team was "the Redskins." I had been approached by one of the local Native American tribes as well as the school. I agreed to see if there was anything I could do to help. There had been protests with confrontations from the White community members and some of the surrounding Native tribes. Emotions ran deep on both sides. The Native Americans wanted the school to change the name of the team. The high school did not want to change it, and neither did the town. The school felt the name was part of the school's seventy-year history. There seemed to be a strange superstition that the name was tied to the team's success. The school had done a survey showing very few of the people there wanted to change the team's name, which is why they had invited me.

One morning, in an auditorium filled with teachers, administrators, and staff, I did a half-day presentation. As soon as I was done with the morning's welcome and introduction, a man stood up. He was sitting in the back corner, where it was difficult for me to see his face. He wanted my personal opinion on what I thought about their need to honor the school's seventy-year history with the team name and mascot. He said the team had a significant legacy tied to that name and he and most of the town agreed they should not change it.

He insisted I give him my personal opinion. I responded by saying, *"You really don't want my opinion; what you really want is the opinion of your colleagues and the people who will have to live with the name after I leave. Your questions are valid and important. A seventy-year legacy is important and needs to be respected, and so does a people's legacy of pain that has gone on for hundreds of years, such as the Native Americans have. Yours is an important question and should be answered by your colleagues at the end of the program."*

I was not there to change his or anyone else's mind. I was there to share information; the changing of mind was up to them. I learned a long time ago I could not change or heal anyone. What I could do was share information to the best of my knowledge. I trust people to do the right thing when confronted with the information they need to fill their information gap. I had done a lot of research on the team and knew they had a long history of winning. During the presentation, they brought that up as an excuse for not changing the name.

I asked them who did the winning, the name or the young people—who put forth their outstanding talent and effort—along with their coaches—who were experts at their crafts—and the parents who supported their children? I asked them if they would allow a different name to change their devotion and dedication to the game? Would they somehow be less if the name of the team were different? Was it the name, or was it the students who were winning the games?

That morning, we watched films focused on Native American history and the history of the name (which by a show of hands no one knew), and we watched a film of the counter-protest that many in the town had participated in. As they watched themselves in action, the silence was palpable. The attack-mob quality of their reaction to the Native Americans peacefully protesting seemed to send a chill down the spines of the participants. The tribe shared a film of the protest with me, and I shared it with them.

When I was finished with the presentation, I asked the group to respond to the question posed by the gentleman in the back of the auditorium earlier that morning. What about the seventy-year legacy the school had with the name? The group was silent for a long time, and then a woman in the front row stood up. She said she did not know most of the history they had been exposed to that day. She felt ashamed of their behavior at the protest. Then another teacher stood up and said, "*The Native American legacy is longer than seventy years; I for one vote to change the name.*" At that point, the man in the back of the room who had asked the original question walked out.

A week later, I got feedback on the evaluations and the new survey. They had had a ninety-seven percent turnaround rate and had voted to change the name. Now they had to convince the town, and they thought that was not going to be easy. My thoughts were, "*You are the town, and if you had a ninety-seven percent turnaround rate, you could at least get fifty-one percent out of the town.*"

I gave them a set of recommendations to help support the town through a series of education programs that included local radio and TV ads. These media spots were to highlight the various ethnic groups in their community and their historical contributions. Their town had a fascinating history of support for the Underground Railroad. That history would be highlighted as well. They loved the recommendations and set up a committee.

The committee decided what they really needed was a White male to help them through the process, not me. This was 2001, and although they were all White and had a ninety-seven percent turnaround rate with my presentation, they thought the town would not listen to a Black woman. Three years after my presentation, they were still fighting over the same issue, and the team's name had not been changed. Denial is what we use to hide from reality and block the truth. It is one of the things we use when we need to make ourselves right.

DENIAL & FEAR OF THE PAST

In September of 2014, students in a Colorado high school protested the changes the school board wanted to make to their history books. The students wanted to stop the censorship of their Advanced Placement History course. The students were asking for honesty in the classroom. The parents claimed the current history is too negative and too violent for them to read. The school board proposal states, in part:

> *Materials should promote citizenship, patriotism, essentials, and benefits of the free enterprise system, respect for authority, and respect for individual rights. Materials should not encourage or condone civil disorder, social strife, or disregard of the law. Instructional materials should present positive aspects of the United States and its heritage.*

Interestingly enough, the students were using civil disobedience to make their case. The school board states, *"AP History casts some parts of our nation's past in a negative light, such as the bombing of Hiroshima and slavery."* The problem with telling only the parts of history that make us look good is it creates a false reality. That type of omission infantilizes us by relegating us to the fantasy land of fairy tales. That kind of omission leads to misinformation, ultimately mystifying us into creating a false sense of self. And those who are misinformed are bound to miscreate.

There are many of these kinds of omissions throughout our history. In Tulsa, Oklahoma, an article was cut out of the bound volumes of the local newspaper in the hopes of covering up one of the biggest race riots in American history—the Tulsa Race Riot of 1921. During seventeen hours of chaos and violence, a White mob attacked a Black community, killed around three hundred African-Americans, looted their homes and businesses, and burned and tore down every building. No White person was ever punished.

The initial reaction of the White leadership immediately following the riot was shame for their behavior. But soon, that changed to a "blame the victim" mentality, and they claimed the community had brought it upon themselves. This community, known as Black Wall Street for the number of Black-owned homes and businesses, was destroyed in one night.

Facing our unpleasant past and the emotions attached to that past is one of America's fears. We've all heard the phrase, or perhaps read the book, "White Fragility," referring to how White people feel about broaching the subject of racism in America. To quote Col. Jessup, played by Jack Nicholson, in the movie *A Few Good Men*: *"You can't handle the truth!"* It is the belief we can't handle the truth that attaches us to the repetitive cycle of our pain and denies us the emotional room to heal. In our desire not to face painful situations, to heal them, we lock ourselves in an unspoken commitment to maintaining the status quo. We sign an invisible contract to a past that, even though we know it does not serve us, is at the very least familiar. Through our collective collusion, we tell ourselves we don't really have a problem and thus deny our need for healing.

If in a moment of grace, we can admit there is something wrong, we quickly defend our position by calling on an experience that will allow us to fuse something in our psyche that will resemble the healed self. These are things like, "*There are many Blacks in positions of power today. The rest of them should just stop complaining and get on the bandwagon,*" or, "*As a Black person in America, I have never experienced any kind of racial discrimination.*" Meanwhile, if you probe deeper, you find the hidden pain that has been suppressed in order to survive. The need to defend our position is one of the surest ways to detect our denial.

Over time, many White people have believed "America does not have an issue of race" that needs to be healed. So, they would just go along floating on the river of denial until something that is race-related happens in the country. Then they and the members of various racial groups swim breathlessly to their individual side of the racial river of denial. Time after time, what might have been a human issue suddenly becomes a racial problem charged with unhealed racial emotions and feelings. When we are unhealed, we always head for our most significant wounds.

Though most of us would rather deny it, race is America's greatest wound, and it will continue to be if we don't muster up the courage to face the past honestly. We need to acknowledge the painful emotions affiliated with our country's errors and commit to healing. If you don't believe America has an unhealed issue with race, just look at what happened during Hurricane Katrina and the aftermath of that disaster.

During the hurricane, babies were separated from their mothers. One thousand five hundred children were missing; not presumed dead, but simply missing. These are children who were separated from their parents by those who were supposed to be helping. The insensitive ways in which people were treated, the length of time it took to get food and water to them, and how people were criminalized, though they were the victims of a natural disaster, is a painful reminder that there is much work to be done if we are to heal from our collective racial pain and shame.

DENIAL SERVES US

In an interesting way, our socialization process requires we make denial part of our survival. We often ignore painful situations and feelings of discomfort for the sake of not being the one who rocks the boat, so we learn to go along to get along. It is easier to collude with a system or situation that does not honor our totality than it is to admit our experience has been embarrassing, offensive, painful, or victimizing. It is easier to suffer in silence than to admit we have a situation before us that is unacceptable.

In an attempt to create the illusion of peace in our lives, we leave issues unaddressed that can be detrimental to ourselves, our families, our organizations, our communities, and indeed, our world. In denial, we ignore and sometimes substitute the intuitive, giving more credence to the cognitive, rather than using both or knowing when to put one over the other. In this lack of balance, we ignore the gut feeling that something needs to be addressed in our lives, and instead of facing whatever it may be, we go on blindly telling ourselves nothing is wrong or it will pass if we just ignore it.

In 2002, in one of my Race Demystified seminars, Mr. Jackson, an African-American man in his late sixties, watched a film of the Tulsa Race Riot. He was visibly shaken. As he shared, he began to cry. He spoke about the death of Emmett Till. Emmett Till was a teenager who had been lynched for whistling at a White woman in the South. His mother had sent him from Chicago to spend the summer with family. Mr. Jackson, a teenager himself at the time when Emmett Till was killed, spoke about looking at the pictures in *Jet Magazine* and realized at that moment he just wasn't safe. He said he realized his parents could not keep him safe, his community could not keep him safe, and the police would not keep him safe. As he sat and cried, he said he had lived a lifetime never, ever feeling safe. He said he had never verbalized that before. It was just a feeling he lived with, an undercurrent that was part of his life. Denial is a story that sits just under the surface of our psyche. This man had lived in the shadow of his lack of safety, and lack of safety can lead to distrust. In his sharing, he found there were other African-American men in the group who had felt the same way. Mr. Jackson said he appreciated their sharing and it helped him feel less alone in the world. Black and Brown people often deny their emotional pain because they feel like, "*What's the point? No one can help me.*"

The problem is denial does not change the situation, nor does it allow the wisdom of discernment that comes from being fully awake, fully alive, and fully present. Denial serves us since, in our ignorance, we feel no responsibility to do anything about that which we deny. In denial, we are always innocent while the rest of the world is seen as guilty. As someone shared in a function I once attended, *"All you need to know about me is I'm perfect and you're not."* We all laughed with this person's introduction of themselves. We laughed because, in a way, it was a silent belief about the world a lot of us seem to share. After all, if everyone were like me, the world would not have a problem, and clearly, neither would I.

In denial, we don't have the wisdom to pick our fights. A great deal of our energy is spent denying there may be a side to the story we've not yet heard, been exposed to, or even considered. For instance, denial leads White men to blame Blacks and People of Color for taking their jobs, when in reality, they don't have the power to do that. The people who have taken your jobs away are those with the power and resources to ship your jobs overseas in search of greater profits while raising the cost of living in your own country. If White men stopped to really look at their whiteness, they would realize the privilege they counted on for generations didn't look like it used to; they might stop blaming those who didn't create the problem in the first place. Discernment helps us out of denial.

In denial, we silently insist the world beyond our filters is virtually nonexistent, so if it's not part of our personal experience, it's not happening at all.

So, denial becomes the great excuse for working on the trivial and external without taking a long hard look inside. While we continue to work hard at our jobs to provide our children with every comfort and amenity, and we are good, well-meaning citizens who attend PTA meetings and serve our communities, we have trouble acknowledging Johnny is dying of his unaddressed emotional overload. Our personal, untapped emotions and fears—not to mention his—eat away at Johnny until he finally cracks, and we wonder how this could have happened. *"This is such a nice community, and Johnny was such a nice boy!"*

It's challenging to help our families resolve emotional issues when we never learned how to work through our own. It's not that we are uncaring parents; we simply didn't learn how. Sometimes the simple honesty of admitting we don't know how to handle something can go a long way with our children. Sometimes in trying to protect our parental ego, we forget the power of our children's love for us. No matter how angry they get with our sometimes-inept way of dealing with them, they love us as much as we love them. Sometimes they have information that can help us help them solve their issues. But so often, we fail to ask the person with the problem what their needs might be.

This seems remarkably close to the way we look to solve community and global problems. We never ask what the community might need. We simply go in with our solutions, looking to solve problems that, by virtue of our lack of experience and missing historical background, we simply do not understand.

In the end, we discover what we really deny is our oneness, that delicate interconnection we have with all living things. Denial allows us the luxury of temporarily believing any experience that does not touch us personally belongs to "them" and not to "us." Denial allows us to believe it's always about them and never about us.

AND WE THINK WE ARE ABOVE IT ALL

It was midsummer, 1994. I was visiting a friend in the UK, and we went to the beach. It was a cold and windy day, and besides the two of us, there was only one other person in sight. He was parasailing in a wetsuit. The sky was grey, and the water a reflection of the colorless sky. A few months later, I was with friends in the Caribbean in the middle of the winter. We had hired a boat to take us to one of the islands dotting Puerto Rico's coast. The sky was blue, the sun was bright, the turquoise water was clear, and dolphins were escorting us to our new destination. For some reason, my mind took me to the grey sky of my European day at the beach.

I thought about what it must have been like for people to cross the ocean for weeks and months, leaving behind the grey skies and dark waters. Suddenly, I became present again to the beauty and the warmth of the moment when I started seeing green rising out of the water in the distance. Eventually, that green was followed by the sand of the beach before us. I stood up to get a better look, and it looked like a jewel rising out of the water. As the island became more visible and the birds flew overhead, this strange feeling came over me. I wanted to own that island. I don't know where that feeling came from, but at that moment, I felt as the so-called explorers might have felt, and I could not judge them in the same way again. I do not condone what they did; I simply became aware it was in me. I wasn't above it. It was a moment of great humility. Denying our shadow doesn't heal it. It simply masks it.

Denial keeps us from looking too deeply into situations. It allows us to send pennies per month to starving children in various parts of the world without needing to understand why they see so little of the wealth produced by their nations. We tell ourselves famine is killing millions a year since people can't grow food without water, while in New York City, we import food from around the world. Somehow, we always manage to get the food to the people who can pay for it with dollars and cents. Those who pay for it with their labor somehow seem less deserving of the crops they grow to feed the world.

One of the most insidious forms of denial takes is our unwillingness to admit how our conditioning influences our lives. We often keep the truth hidden from ourselves because there's guilt or ancestral shame affiliated with a particular circumstance. Anyone who wants to understand how engrained race is as a form of separation in our society, and how much influence this conditioning has on our daily lives, simply needs to engage in a simple exercise:

PART 1

On a piece of paper, create a timeline of your experiences with race. Start by dividing your timeline into ages, such as one year to five years of age, six years to ten years of age, eleven years to fifteen years of age, and continue to your current age. After you have done this, give yourself five minutes of reflection time. Reflect on these questions:

While you were growing up, what personal experiences did you have? What statements did you hear about people of various races?

You may have heard these things from parents, grand-parents, siblings, teachers, friends, politicians, and clergy; it could be personal experiences. Close your eyes if it helps you focus. Give yourself the full five minutes. If your mind wanders, it's okay; this is not an exercise that comes easily for many of us. Let yourself refocus and stay with it for the full five minutes. When the five minutes are up, write down anything you remember. You may write it in as little or as much detail as you like. When you are finished, take a deep breath, and look at what you have written.

PART 2

This is the empowering side of the exercise. On a separate piece of paper, create a timeline of your empowering experiences with race. Start by dividing your timeline into ages, such as one year to five years of age, six years to ten years of age, eleven years to fifteen years of age, and continue to your current age. After you have done this, give yourself five minutes of reflection time. Reflect on this question:

While you were growing up, what empowering statements did you hear about the various races?

Repeat the first part of the exercise. Take a deep breath. Put both of your timelines together and compare the two. Which timeline has the most information?

Which part of your conditioning are you most likely to unconsciously act out of—your derogatory racial conditioning or your empowering racial conditioning?

What we learned well and experienced most will color our experiences of the world and our relationships with others. If what we learned was fear-based, our relationships will be based on that fear. If what we learned was love, then that will be the guiding light to our experiences. Denial of our personal history can be detrimental to the healing process.

Denial is an integral part of what keeps racism in place. Take a deep breath and let's dig deeper. In the next chapter, we will continue our exploration of denial.

QUESTIONS TO CONSIDER:

- Where do you see racial denial in our national discourse?

- What did you learn about denial from your family?

- How is racial denial serving you?

CHAPTER 22

DENIAL MAINTAINS DYSFUNCTION

―――

"Denial ain't just a river in Egypt."

—MARK TWAIN

In polite society, if we're to be seen as respectable, trustworthy citizens, emotions are things we are to leave outside the door. Yet, our emotions are precisely what we will have to access if we are to heal from our internalized racial conditioning. Denial of our feelings and emotions becomes a way of life on which our very safety is hinged. Yet, there is something about denial that carries with it an inherent sense of guilt. Denial stands firmly on the premise there is something we are not admitting to for whatever reason. More often than not, the reason is emotional safety. Denial keeps us in our place with a false sense of safety that eats away at the very fabric of our core.

Denial is an essential piece of the dysfunctional puzzle and one on which the dysfunction itself depends. It is part of an elaborately constructed safety mechanism built on fear of the truth and held together by shame and guilt. It leads us to feel attacked by anyone who threatens to expose us and our personal stance of defense to this very personal attack, which becomes emotional fight, flight, or paralysis. There are times when we are grateful to be awakened from our denial, but for the most part, we shoot the messenger.

Our fundamental nature is one of truth. When we surround ourselves with false statements, false realities, and false safety, we live in a constant state of fear. Life becomes a kind of *"hope that no one finds me out,"* a sure sign we are not living from our truth. A simple question or suggestion is seen as a threat to that which we are consciously or unconsciously trying to deny. And in defense of our safety, we often attack anyone who dares to pull us from the sanctum of our self-constructed wall.

Denial allows us to say, "There *but* for the Grace of God go I." Perhaps we should consider changing that statement to: "There go I." This might awaken us to the fact we are all in this together. Unfortunately, *"but"* is a separating word.

Denial is neither right nor wrong, good nor bad. Denial need not be judged, but simply looked at for its effect on our lives. The truth is we all experience denial in one form or another. Denial can be a privilege allotted to those whose lives are not personally touched by specific circumstances. While drugs were a problem in Latino and African-American neighborhoods for years, America did not have a drug problem. The moment drugs became a problem in middle- and upper-middle-class suburban Americans, those with power and money declared war on drugs. They blamed the Black and Brown community for the drugs that were infiltrating the White neighborhoods. The war on drugs put men and women in jail who should have gone to rehab to be treated for their disease.

Denial allowed us all to view terrorism around the world from the virtual safety of our living rooms for years. In our own country, we have historically watched as hate groups of all beliefs terrorized Jews, African-Americans, Latinos, Native Americans, Asians, gay men, lesbians, and transgender members of our communities while claiming terrorism exists in other countries but not here. When terrorism finally hit home through the planes crashing into the World Trade Center buildings, we declared a war on terrorism. In my own curiosity, I wonder if it will be as successful as our war on drugs. It's a funny thing about wars; they are most often waged on effects and not cause. It's the old adage of fighting violence with violence without ever asking what caused the violence in the first place. Perhaps the question is, "*What makes so many people feel they need to take drugs?*" To quote Henry David Thoreau, "*There are a thousand hacking at the branches of evil to one who is striking at the root.*"

I remember a woman coming up to me after a presentation at an international conference where I had just spoken on racism in America. I was speaking with a colleague in the breezeway leading to the hotel lobby. As she approached us, my friend and I expanded our circle to include her. She began to speak of how powerful the presentation had been for her. She said seeing my colleague and I standing in conversation reminded her of an experience she'd had a few years prior. This woman happened to be staying at a hotel that was hosting a conference for African-American women. She recalled a group of women in a circle who seemed to be enjoying each other's company. Her words spoke of feeling very drawn to that group of women. She wanted to join them;

there seemed to be such camaraderie between them. I asked why she didn't join them. She said they were strangers and might not have appreciated her joining in. Fear of rejection is a natural human experience.

She then added she had noticed there seemed to be a sisterhood between Black women that White women simply did not share. I thought that was an interesting comment but decided to let her finish; I sensed something else at play. My experiences with these kinds of encounters had taught me about our need to be heard without being judged. Our willingness to be candid about our personal experiences is an essential first step in dismantling denial.

The woman continued by talking about how she would love to have African-American women friends, but she did not know how to approach the friendship. She said she hated how we were all separated from one another and wished we could just have normal relationships. In her words, *"I hate all of this racial stuff, and I wish I could do something about it."*

Enthusiastically, I suggested she find an Institute for the Healing of Racism in her native state and join. My suggestion came from what I heard as a genuine plea to be part of one human family. Her response came back quickly and loaded. Her eyes filled with tears as she said, *"Are you saying I'm a racist? Do I sound like a racist? What did I say that made you think that I'm a racist?"* Shocked by her response, I simply looked at her with a mixture of compassion and loss of patience. My colleague responded by saying, *"She has not accused you of anything. She simply suggested a place you might find some of what you are looking for."* I went on to speak about the institutes and the oneness of humanity. When I thought our conversation was over, we said our goodbyes and my colleague and I began to walk away.

After a few moments, the woman chased after us and said, "*I need to tell you one more thing.*" Her story went like this:

> *When I was a little girl,*" she began, "*I lived with my grandparents. They loved me dearly, and I would have done anything to please them.* I watched as she openly began to cry. *I was six years old and used to walk to school past an orphanage,* she added, *and there was a little Black girl who I used to walk to school with every day. We were friends, and one day during dinner, I told my grandparents about my new friend. It was my birthday, and I wanted her to come. I told them we walked to school together every morning. My grandparents looked at each other and said, "Honey, I would not do that if I were you. We don't want you walking with her anymore." The next day, I crossed the street when I saw her coming out of the orphanage. After that, I never spoke to her again.*

I let her finish her story and held her, letting her cry in my arms. My friend joined, and all three of us cried. We cried for her loss and ours. We cried for broken friendships and broken trust. We cried for goodbyes that were never said and explanations that were never given. We cried for that child who was left to wonder what happened. For more than half a century, this woman carried this wound that kept her separate, not entirely understanding why as an adult she found it so hard to have African-American female friends. The denial of her racial wound put her in situations where she felt awkward. In her desperate search for the politically correct thing to do and say, she could not reach her heart to connect honestly and lovingly with another human being because of the color of their skin. Denial keeps us from accessing the truth of our interconnectedness.

Along with this woman's pain was the pain of another woman. The child who used to walk with her to school had been painfully rejected. She was not offered the benefit of an explanation. At that age, she might have suspected her rejection had racial overtones, or perhaps not. Still, no matter what the cause, rejection is a painful experience most of us carry throughout our lives. Rejection is one of our universal fears.

Every time we are wounded, it's as if a wooden dagger has been driven through our hearts. The deeper the wound, the more likely we are to deny our association with it. The memory of the pain creates a living hell that denial helps us escape. We all know how painful it is to remove something embedded in us, yet that is precisely what we must do if we are to heal.

In graphic terms, the skin that grows around the blade helps us keep it in place. We ignore it, telling ourselves it does not hurt or even that it does not exist. We walk around protecting the pain, lest anyone touch it or push it even deeper. We build a system of defenses around the pain that keeps us from having to remove it. In short, we become addicted to our denial the dagger even exists, and as with all addictions, we do what we have to do to maintain it, keeping the discomfort and our addiction to it firmly in place.

We live our lives in protective mode, hoping no one will notice we are hiding something painful. From this position of defense, we see others as our potential attackers, no matter how innocent they may be. The energy used up in defending and keeping our dysfunction in position leaves us weak and defenseless. Our energy is spent on keeping others from seeing the wound, lest they use it against us.

We know we could heal the wound, but that would mean removing the blade, and we all know how painful that would be. It would mean admitting something is wrong and peeling back the layers of denial we have built to hold the dysfunction firmly in place. Removal causes bleeding, pain, and tears. It means a wound will have to be opened again so all that has accumulated to keep it in place can be cleaned out. It means exposing the wound to fresh air and medication that will keep it from getting infected. It means dedication and work, and attention to something from which we spent a great deal of time hiding. It means mustering the courage to do whatever we need to do to stay on the healthy side of our wound. It means having patience and compassion toward the self and others while the wound heals.

This woman had learned separation was a way of protecting the pain and guilt she felt for separating from a child who had not hurt her in any way. Although she desired to join, become friends with, and have warm and caring relationships with women, regardless of their skin color, she felt restricted in her choice of friends. Moreover, she feared the rejection she had inflicted upon that child would be mirrored back to her by women who looked like the child she had once rejected.

In our denial, we fail to acknowledge children may not always do as we say, but they will do as we do. They see us socialize with people who look like us. We live next door to people who look like us and go to church with people who look like us. The people we work with primarily look like us, and the people we call our friends and who we celebrate life with and sit at our dinner parties with look just like us. Why are we so surprised when our children socialize just like us? Such are the virtues of our denial; it keeps us from seeing how our actions affect the people around us. Denial keeps us from moving past the experiences to look at the probable causes.

When we choose to heal our denial, we suddenly find we are exhausted from upholding the burden of maintaining a false sense of safety. Without denial, we have the energy to access the truth of our feelings—the anger, rage, and disappointment that lies just beneath the surface of our denial. Denial of our racial conditioning is a dagger that has wounded all of us in one form or another. And it is the first layer that must be dismantled if we are to heal and have lasting peace.

Still, dismantling denial is a tall order because we believe in its own way, it has kept us safe. When the psychological pain is greater than we can bear, denial serves us well. It allows us to function in an otherwise dysfunctional environment. But to heal, we must get out of denial. The exit points directly to the next door that leads to anger. What we learned about anger from early on it is simply not allowed. So, how do we get out of our collective denial?

Getting out of denial means accepting something is not quite right. It means facing the feelings of pain, discomfort, and betrayal that come with that acceptance. Denial serves us in reconciling what we know in our hearts to be true with an external experience that is different from that which is in our hearts. The heart, intuition, and inner knowing are our sacred connections to our fundamental innocence and wisdom. We know when our actions are out of sync with our basic nobility and goodness. Denial keeps us repeating patterns of behavior that do not allow us to access the wisdom of the heart. It leaves us vulnerable to passersby who make innocent and sometimes not-so-innocent remarks. It triggers unconscious behavior governed by that which we are denying.

Denial is a great thief. It robs us of our inherent right to heal. If we ever allow ourselves passage through the painful corridors of denial, we find what we defended so vehemently was our right to live in fear—the fear of having simple, loving relationships with other members of *our human race.*

Even our bodies recognize denial and react by giving us a jolt in the stomach that cannot be ignored. This jolt is often the trigger of the fight-or-flight effect, which leads us to defend ourselves verbally or physically. We are so ingrained in all we have learned about race in the last four hundred years that we've built a personal shrine to our conditioning, which we worship to in the form of addiction, and we're not even aware of all we'll do to defend it.

BREAKING THE CYCLE

There is such a thing as the right use of denial. To deny we are less than what we truly are is the proper use of denial. To choose not to accept labels or inappropriate names is the correct use of denial. To deny the things we are not is the right use of denial. How do we break the cycle of denial?

Recognition: When presented with a person, action, or idea that pushes your proverbial racial button, ask yourself why that was so disturbing to you. Remember Resmaa Menakem's words: *"If it's hysterical, it's historical."* If it's triggering you, you have a history with it. What was it about that comment that triggered you to want to defend yourself? Instead of blaming another, ask what you might be denying within yourself that caused your reaction. See every need to defend yourself as an opportunity to heal a conscious or unconscious wound. This wound may or may not have anything to do with what you are experiencing at that moment.

Honest Appraisal: Racial healing requires an honest appraisal, a personal truth, and racial reconciliation with our history so we might understand our conditioning. History gives us the context and allows for a deeper understanding of our current events. When we go to the doctor to be treated for an ailment, the first thing the medical staff does is get an accurate account of our medical history. This history gives the health care staff information that helps them understand what might be happening to us, what to look for, and possibly even how to treat it. A missing or inaccurate historical account makes it more difficult, if not impossible, to accurately diagnose what may be happening with the patient now. This makes it impossible to determine what the patient needs to heal.

In this respect, the healing of ourselves, our relationships, our communities, and our world require no less than our doctor requires for our healing. An honest appraisal based on our individual and collective histories is key to our healing. This means all the stories get told, both the pleasant and the not-so-pleasant ones. It means we open our eyes to the biases of our conditioning by looking at our personal images of good and bad and how these images were formed.

Honest appraisal means we look at things with the clear objectivity of a well-informed mind and a compassionate and open heart that desires not to judge, but simply to understand. It allows every member of the problem an opportunity to speak the truth, from their experience, with the safety of knowing they will not be crucified for the telling. An honest appraisal helps us to understand we are all in this together and it is together we must come if we are ever to heal.

Acceptance: This is accepting we have all learned survival patterns but we are not inextricably tied to those patterns. Patterns can be changed. This is the key to our healing.

Responsibility: Don't leave your healing in the hands of others. You can't wait for "those people over there" who affect your life to change for you to feel better. Taking personal responsibility for our healing puts us back in control of our lives. We are no longer dependent on the choices others make, nor are we at the mercy of another's dysfunction. Taking personal responsibility for our own racial healing allows us to choose how to respond to situations and experiences. It enables compassionate honesty with others and ourselves. It keeps us from attacking and defending and gives us an opportunity to choose healthy, positive actions that lead to freedom and peace. In short, actions we can live with.

Action: Right action can be easily recognized by the way it makes us feel. Right action carries with it a sense of lasting peace and a knowing that we can live with ourselves once it's all over. In the case of racial denial, right action is opening ourselves up to another's experiences without blaming or judging ourselves or others. Remember, we are all in this together. If we are ever to access truth, we must be willing to listen to all sides without diminishing another's experience.

As we listen, watch, or read about different experiences, we need to pay attention to feelings and emotions as they arise and be present with our fight or flight responses. Notice how you feel in your body. Sitting quietly with feelings is not easy, but when the cause of those feelings is unmasked, it represents one less button that can be pushed within us. It means the dagger that kept us from healing has been pulled out, and our wound finally has an opportunity to heal. Our healing frees vast amounts of energy that can help us on our way to the next level in our journey of transformation.

QUESTIONS TO CONSIDER:

- How does your family do racial denial?

- How do your coworkers do racial denial?

- Why do you do racial denial?

- How does racial denial serve you?

- How would moving out of racial denial serve you?

Once we move out of denial, we often go into anger. Are you angry about racism? In the next stage of the Healer's Code, we will look at anger.

CHAPTER 23

STAGE 4
ANGER

ANGER AND THE ARCHETYPE
OF THE WARRIOR

*"I shall allow no man to belittle my
soul by making me hate him."*

BOOKER T. WASHINGTON

I have always been passionate about my work, but I did not
know the depth of my anger until I started working on my
pain. As activists, we are often driven by our anger. We don't
always realize there is a fine line between our passion and our
anger, and we don't pay attention to the energy that drives
us. For my work in helping people recover from racial conditioning to be effective, I needed to be discerning between
those two emotions. I learned anger is a feeling born from
having been wronged, violated, denied, and deceived. But
anger holds a lot of energy, and if it is the only thing driving

our work, it can leave us exhausted and even make us sick. Anger can fuel our passions in such a way it consumes us. Moreover, anger can negatively affect the very thing we are looking to heal. It keeps people from hearing us, as the emotion itself can speak louder than our words. Anger needs to be expressed if we are to heal. Our anger needs a safe outlet like punching our pillows, screaming in the woods, or jumping vigorously. Crying also helps.

When it comes to racism, anger is more than justified. The problem is anger is an energy that feeds. It feeds the people around us, it feeds our purpose, and it feeds the very thing we are looking to change. Anger can be detrimental to our causes, as anger invites anger; it keeps us from thinking clearly and gives our power away. But anger is not to be denied. If we are truly going to heal, it is to be embraced and transformed. Anger transformed can be fuel for the journey. As activists, we want to make change happen; we want to make things better; we want a world of peace. We don't realize our anger feeds the opposite of what we are looking to create. While many will disagree, the most effective activists know how to work with the energy of peace. If you don't believe that, read the works of Dr. Martin Luther King Jr., Mahatma Gandhi, and Nelson Mandela.

When I was in the throes of my anger, I thought I would never stop being angry. It seemed the more diligently I worked on my self-recovery, the more anger I uncovered. There were times I felt as if my anger was an abyss from which I would never return. But return I did, with a lighter heart and a renewed sense of purpose. The gift I gained by allowing myself to move through my anger led me to a depth of compassion I know I could not have acquired any other way. This gift restored my heart, allowing me to forgive myself and others and allowing me to feel more loving and complete. I learned to say, *"I'm angry, or I'm hurt, or I'm scared,"* and to know I am safe in my expression. Equally as important, it helped me to understand others are not much different from myself. I faced my anger with God and came to understand free will gave rise to a world that was never meant to be separate and apart from love. Facing my anger helped me to find peace in my own heart, and it helped me to understand we are wired for love.

At times, we don't realize how transparent we really are. People can see through our anger; they can read our anger, even when we think we are masters at hiding it. Years ago, I was interacting with a vendor who spoke of having great admiration for my work. I had only met this woman once prior to this time, and she invited me to an art show where her friend was exhibiting his sculptures. She said he had sculpted a piece that reminded her of me. I thought this was interesting for someone who hardly knew me. I attended the show, and as I walked around the gallery among those beautiful sculptures, there was one piece that took my breath away. I just stared at it. The woman walked up to me and said, *"I see you found it."* The sculpture was of a woman, an angel, made of scrap iron. Her wings were spread open, and she was clearly in flight. Her right arm was extended in front of her, and in her hand she held a sword. The piece was called "The Warrior Angel." Transparent anger is visible to the world, even when it is not visible to us. This woman could see my anger, even when I couldn't. She could feel the war and the warrior in me, as well as the angel.

I had moved from the East Coast to the middle of the country to take a job. I was away from my loving spiritual community, friends, and family. The all-White middle-age-plus male leadership where I worked was looking to transform the racial dynamics in the organizations and communities they served. But something didn't feel right, and that feeling was making me feel unsafe. One day when I returned from lunch, I was stopped by two women who worked for a man who had an office two doors away from mine. They greeted me nervously and pointed to the man's office, saying, "*This is your office now.*"

"*What?*" I was confused!

While I was out to lunch, they had moved all of my personal items to his office because he had decided he liked where I was located better than he liked his own office. I asked, "*Where is he?*"

"*He's off-site doing training.*"

"*Tell him to call me. I'll be at home working until every piece of furniture and every last one of my personal items are moved back to my original office.*" I stayed home three days until my office was put back the way I had it. But this caused a rupture—not just in the working relationship, but also in me.

After that, things were not the same at work. My decision to stand up for myself and ask for what I wanted made me persona non grata. To take my mind off of my work environment, I took up archery and would have competitions with my then-teenage son in our backyard. I was amazed at how good I was with that recurve bow. A friend who was visiting commented on my accuracy and suggested I put my workmate's photo on the bullseye. I was horrified at the idea of using a human face as an actual target. But at that moment, I realized I was using archery to release anger, and my anger stemmed from not feeling safe. There was something ancient, something primal about using that bow and arrow. Something about it seemed familiar.

When we begin our process, we can often see we hold more of the warrior in us than of the peacemaker. We are passionate about our activism, and we mask the anger with our passion. Still, the anger must be worked through if we are going to be the living example of what we really want: peace.

I was spending a weekend at an inn in Vermont with Camelia Sadat. She often spoke of her father, Nobel Peace Prize winner and former president of Egypt, Anwar el-Sadat. She said her father told her he was a great proponent of war until he walked a battlefield filled with dead young men. The shock and horror turned him into a peacemaker. Camelia spoke of the trauma of seeing her father killed on television while making a speech. Ultimately, activists are here to create a better world, a world of greater peace and equity. To do so effectively, we need to work through our own anger. We are not here to poison the well. We are here to clear its waters, and to do so, we must delve into the shadow of our pain, whether it be caused by our family or our society.

Anger draws people to protest, and protests can be peaceful, or they can turn to a riot where innocent people who showed up to express their feelings can be hurt or killed. The reason people fear anger so much is someone else's anger can get us killed. When people are in deep anger, they are often irrational, making it hard to trust them. Unexpressed anger spills over on to everything we do, from slamming dishes at the dinner table to abusing family members to the burning of Black Wall Street in 1921 to storming the US Capitol in 2021.

There is nothing wrong with anger as long as we don't make it the driving force of our lives. We can always find a way to get back to love. The move toward harmonious relationships with all humanity should be the goal. In the meantime, find something loving to move toward.

HEALING AND DEALING WITH EMOTIONS

WHAT'S ALL THAT ANGER ABOUT?

Emotions and feelings are two of those things our society finds difficult to deal with, yet accessing emotions is an integral part of the healing process, and it's imperative to the healing of racism.

While anger and frustration are not emotions we want to hang on to, expressing these feelings is an important part of the healing process. From early childhood, we are taught to repress anger. We are not allowed to rage or yell or scream when we feel we have been wronged. For most people, anger is the least popular and the most frightening of all emotions.

When it comes to race, anger is the most loaded of all emotions. People on all sides of the issue are angry. People of Color are angry for a million and one obvious reasons, all of which we have heard before. White people are angry because they don't understand what all the fuss is about. In short, no one is happy. To make things more frustrating, institutionalized racism and internalized conditioning of oppression and privilege keep a keg of dynamite between the various groups, needing only the match of a community incident to be ignited.

To be angry means you are no longer in denial of the injustices we've experienced and the lies that have been told to us to keep us ignorant, thereby making us easier to control. While anger may be a difficult stage, it is unhealthy not to allow ourselves the full expression of this emotion. I remember when I was moving through the thickest part of my anger. It was as if I had fallen into a well I would never climb out of. But eventually, I did, and I emerged calmer, more willing to be patient with myself and others, and more open to allowing others their process.

Most of us grew up in a culture that is afraid of anger, and that fear keeps us trapped in it. Anger, like any other emotion, is a gift of expression, and like any other emotion, it can be used or misused. Healthy use of anger can lead us to take healthy action in our lives. Anger can lead us to say "*no more*" to abusive situations and painful experiences. If we are to heal from racism, anger must be expressed. It is part of the grief we feel from all the losses racism incurs. Anger expressed in healthy ways can lead to breakthroughs and creative realizations. Anger is a natural part of the healing process.

QUESTIONS TO CONSIDER:

- What about racism makes you angry? Be specific.

- How do you act and react when you're angry?

- How can you use your anger in positive ways?

- How do you take care of yourself when you're angry?

- How do you react when others are angry with you?

- Does other people's anger frighten you?

Because we are afraid of our anger and the anger of others, we go into the next stage, which is bargaining.

CHAPTER 24

STAGE 5
BARGAINING

———

FACING THE WHEELER DEALER

*"Have the courage to face a difficulty lest it
kick you harder than you bargain for."*

KING STANISLAUS I

Bargaining is one of the first things we learn. In common language, bargaining simply states, *"If I (fill in your own words), then I…" "If I this, then I that." "If I cry, I get fed. If I cry, I get my diaper changed. If I cry, I'll get held."* Bargaining is the simple act of cause and effect based on personal control. It is negotiation to make change happen.

Perhaps because of the simplicity of the language of bargaining, we get very good at it very quickly. By the time we are three years old, we are quite good at negotiation to have our needs met. A simple trip to the grocery store can be a clear illustration as the three-year-old looks longingly into the adult's eyes and asks, *"If I'm very good while you shop, can I get a candy bar?"* The intellectual challenge of *"I don't have a manual for being a parent"* type of inexperience can be obvious even to the rather competent *"I don't need a manual to know how to manipulate you"* three-year-old.

We get so excited at the prospect of not being embarrassed by a screaming child in the middle of the store that without thinking, we agree. We go along with the child to get along with the child, and our momentary relief can later become a nightmare. That bargained for candy can keep the three-year-old awake when we want them to sleep. Overtired, with eyes that won't close, the child screams their head off. In the moment, we forget we got what we bargained for—peace and quiet in the store—and we should really be grateful. Isn't this what we wanted, peace in the moment? That was the bargaining chip. The child said they'd be quiet in the store. They kept their word. They said nothing about what would happen after that, and you did not give a second thought to the consequences of the greater part of the bargain. In shortsightedness, we solve the momentary problem at the expense of the long-term experience. This was one of my first lessons as a young parent.

In the meantime, the child learned something very valuable. Bargaining works! So, we keep doing it. By the time we are teenagers, we are great at it. *"If I keep my room clean, can I get the keys to the car on Saturday?"* *"If I do all my chores, can I get a raise in my allowance?"* *"If I get in with the right crowd, then I'll be popular. If I wear the right clothes, then I'll be seen."* On and on, we bargain for things, some of which are valuable, some of which are not.

Like everything else, bargaining is neither good nor bad, right or wrong. Bargaining in and of itself elicits no judgments. It's how we use bargaining that can either support us or destroy us. We bargain so much we do it without being aware of what we are doing, and that can be dangerous. Our proficiency with bargaining turns us into unconscious bargainers, and we sometimes give away parts of ourselves we hold dear.

When it comes to the issue of race, we bargain and rationalize. Instead of insisting on equal education for all, we move our children to the "right" school system. Instead of insisting on better housing for all, we lock ourselves behind gated communities. As long as life is better for us, we can extend our charity to those people over there. Just keep them away from here. The only problem is gates imprison those within as much as it keeps "those people" out. Gates, forts, motes, and walls are synonymous with fear. And in fear, no one is living in their light.

BARGAINING FOR DEI

After the civil rights movement, when American companies began opening their doors to more African-Americans than they had in previous decades, something began to happen. Suddenly, people who lived in racial segregation became each other's peers. The friction and strain of the racial caste living began to show. Organizations came up with the idea of "sensitivity training" as a way of relieving tensions between Black and White employees. By the 1970s as this training began to take hold, the women's movement was strengthening, and more women were entering the labor market. Gay rights were coming to the forefront as well. By the 1980s, marginalized groups began to cry out for equal rights. As a way of appeasing all groups, diversity training came into play. By the 1990s, organizations came up with the idea of being more inclusive of all groups by calling what was known as sensitivity training, diversity training. Eventually the name changed to "diversity" and "inclusion" training. So, race took a back seat as organizations tried to show all employees they mattered. Many organizations thought by dealing with diversity in an inclusive way, they were taking care of "the race problem."

Around 2010, organizations finally realized race had to be dealt with as a separate topic, but it was still not to be dealt with head-on. So, they came up with Diversity, Equity, and Inclusion (DEI). This avoided using the word race, and it kept people from complaining that we were dealing with the race issue again and there were other issues in the organization that required just as much attention. Then, in May of 2020, George Floyd was murdered by then-policeman Derek Chauvin, and everything changed. Organizations are more open to treating race as a separate subject. They are more curious and less willing to bargain. They're beginning to understand what their Black and Brown employees deal with on a regular basis. After years of bargaining, we are now open to be more aware of the impact of race on all of us.

Good negotiations require people speak the same language, or at least that they use a translator. In the language of racial conditioning, we need to be aware people speak through their filters acquired through our caste system. No matter which way you turn it, negotiating to avoid dealing directly with the race conversation does not work. We can no longer afford to bargain our way out of dealing with race and racism in our families, communities, or nation.

QUESTIONS TO CONSIDER:

- When it comes to racism, where are you bargaining?

- Are you negotiating to stay in ignorance and asleep?

- Where in your racial pattern are you not willing to bargain?

- When it comes to race and racism, are you willing to negotiate for justice and equity?

CHAPTER 25

STAGE 6

DEPRESSION

---

*"The trauma of oppression leaves a lingering
aftermath. On the surface, we feel the fear; we
just don't remember what caused it."*

—MILAGROS PHILLIS

The fear we feel growing up in limiting situations with limiting
beliefs can be detrimental to our wellbeing. Fear is not the
cause; fear is the effect of being oppressed and traumatized.
It's what happens when a system drains the spirit of liberation that is the very essence of a human's rights. We fear for
ourselves, we fear others, and we fear for others. We become
frightened of the dangers and threats posed by oppressive
systems. It is important to remember systems, laws, families,
or anything requiring allegiance through fear are systems of
oppression that are counter to human nature. A system that
is successful through the use of fear is draining the lifeblood
of its followers, and its success is costing us in human power,

productivity, and the lifting of society. Oppression becomes depression, not just emotional, but physical, intellectual, and economical. One day, we wake up to a society that is medicated both legally and illegally from the children to the elderly. We don't dig for a root cause; we just look for the societal pill we believe will make things better. But of course, that pill fails, so we look for another and another and another until we find ourselves addicted.

White people's allegiance to racism and the ills it propels keeps them living in an unconscious and conscious fear of reprisal, from the fear of the revolt to fear of saying the wrong thing. Moreover, White fear keeps People of Color living like runaway slaves. We see it in stop and frisk, driving while Black, birdwatching while Black, and sitting in Starbucks while Black. We see it in the distribution of mortgages and loans. We see it in the distribution of school funding, which is directly tied to housing prices. We see it in the endless micro- and macroaggressions People of Color experience at work.

"Your biography becomes your biology."

—CAROLINE MYSS

We can't heal the socioemotional depression of racism through medication and denial. The best medication can do is to numb us long enough to remain functional. If we are to heal, we need to understand racism's cause and effect and determine we are not our depression or our oppression. Who we are is so much more than any disease or dysfunction that assails us, social, or otherwise.

Social oppression is what happens when we live without hope, and we live without hope when the systems that seem to be bigger than us don't deliver the freedom, justice, and compassion that are professed in the stories we tell ourselves and others. Depression is the pain of the discrepancy between what we know in our hearts to be true and the dysfunction of our existence. Depression happens when we deny other humans what we see as our natural right or when we control through physical, emotional, psychological, or economic violence. Social oppression is an invisible affliction we carry with great shame. We see it in the ways individuals deny their relationships to groups they see as oppressed, such as denial of Black relatives in the Latino-Hispanic community. We give oppression different names, such as racism, sexism, and all the other '-isms' that exist in our global community, but in the end, it's really oppression we are talking about.

Depressed is the "never going to" stage. It's never going to look any different; it's never going to get better; it's never going to end. When it comes to race, you hear people say, "*Oh, it's never going to change.*" If people don't get good information, it's not. Things can change, but for that to happen, people must change.

When people get different information from what they previously had, they can choose to make different decisions. When people get good information, they make good decisions. We've all had a lot of bad information about race. While there are people in the world who are so wounded that they think they can do no more than wound others, most people want to do the right thing. They just don't know what to do.

OPPRESSION DEPRESSION & GRIEF

The prolonged grief caused by racial oppression can become depression. We walk through the stages of grief, unconscious, self-conscious, or conscious. We often experience unconscious grief as a feeling of sadness. We don't even know why; there's just this incredible sadness we can't seem to shake. We don't even know where the sadness is coming from. It just feels like we are mourning for something, but we don't know what. The mind, body, and emotions are grieving, but there's nothing in our lives we can point to that may be causing the sadness. Someone outside of us—a friend or a loved one—may suddenly ask, *"Are you okay?"* They see something's off, but you're not necessarily aware you're grieving. You suddenly burst into tears, and at the moment, the grief becomes conscious. You are aware of the grief and its prolonged aftermath of depression.

Self-conscious depression is when you know you're depressed and don't want anyone to know you're depressed. You know you're self-conscious when you become annoyed at people who point out your depression. Seek professional help. While finding a good therapist who is racially aware and conscious may not be easy, it is a good idea to keep seeking until you find one.

When you have a society that's based on segregation, the body grieves, the mind grieves, and the heart grieves. Human beings were not created to live in isolation from one another. They were created to be communal beings and to live together and find ways to live in harmony. In fact, the human race would not have survived had we not been communal. When you create systems of segregation, what you're doing is creating forms of oppression that don't allow human beings to express themselves in the way they need to in relationships and friendships. No matter what one might think about race and racism, it is counter to human nature. Racism is a social ill and needs to be treated as such.

Institutionalized oppression, or laws established to oppress specific groups of people, depress the whole nation. The US has one of the highest depression rates in the world. According to *US News & World Report*, the US ranks third in depression. *"The US is one of the most depressed countries in the world, according to the World Health Organization. In terms of quality years of life lost due to disability or death—a widely adopted public health metric that measures the overall burden of disease—the US ranked third for unipolar depressive disorders, just after China, which ranked No. 1, and India"* (2016).

Racism is institutionalized oppression. Oppression causes grief, both conscious and unconscious. Prolonged grief causes depression.

Looking at race and racism through Elisabeth Kübler-Ross's stages of death and dying gives us the opportunity to look at what happens when we embrace the wholeness of who we are. What we know about race is a myth we will have to allow to die.

Elisabeth Kübler-Ross worked in hospice, and she noticed people went through a process when they were told they were going to die. The patient would go into denial: *"This can't be me; it must be a wrong diagnosis."* When they realized this was their diagnosis, they would go into anger: *"Why me?"* From there, they would progress into bargaining, negotiation for prolonged life: *"Maybe if I change my diet, maybe I can get better."* For many, the bargain of taking better care of themselves to get different results wouldn't work, and they would get depressed. She noticed many died in depression, but many would accept their plight and, at the acceptance of their mortality, would take action to do the best they could with the time they had. They were willing to make the most out of their situation. Some would reconnect with family; others would travel. Some would write books. The acceptance stage can mobilize one into taking action—often inspired action.

It is easy to get depressed when dealing with racism. It is a longstanding global dysfunction that has taken and continues to take many lives. But if we focus only on what has been, we can get stuck there. When it comes to racism, the best way out of depression is to accept racism is real and something has to change.

QUESTIONS TO CONSIDER:

- Looking at it from the perspective of race and racism, where do you think our nation is in the stages of grief?

- Have you ever felt hopeless or depressed about race and racism? Give an example.

- Have you ever felt overwhelmed by racism?

- Do you have a way of lifting your spirit when you're feeling off-balance, and if so, how?

HEALING

"The wound is the place where the Light enters you."

—RUMI

CHAPTER 26

STAGE 7
ACCEPTANCE

———

"Understanding is the first step to acceptance, and only with acceptance can there be recovery."

—J.K. ROWLING

There was a time when I knew nothing about the history that was driving racism. I didn't know I had been conditioned to see the world through the eyes of segregation. I didn't know I had been lied to. I just didn't understand. I was one of those who came to acceptance kicking and screaming. Acceptance, to me, was a kind of giving up. It felt like, *"Oh well, that's the way things are. Accept it."* But nothing could be further from the truth.

Acceptance is the stage of transition and choice. You can choose to remain as you are, or you can choose to make changes to create new ways of being in your life. Acceptance can be victimizing or empowering. It is here where, if we've not yet done so, we begin to make different choices that come from understanding. Acceptance is the bridge from what was to what can be.

Accepting we have all learned patterns of survival that have allowed us to live in a system of racial dysfunction and we are not inextricably tied to those patterns is part of healing. Patterns can be changed, and this is the key to our healing process. Taking personal responsibility for our healing puts us back in control of our lives. We are no longer dependent on the choices others make, nor are we at the mercy of another's dysfunction. Taking personal responsibility allows us to choose how we will respond to situations and experiences. It allows us compassionate honesty with others and ourselves. It keeps us from attacking and defending and gives us an opportunity to choose healthy, positive actions that lead to freedom and peace—in short, actions we can live with.

Racism will not be wiped from our world while we're healing. However, healing can help us change our actions, reactions, and interactions. Right action can be easily recognized by the way it makes us feel. Right action carries with it a sense of lasting peace and a knowing that we are sovereign over our emotions. Remember, we are all in this together.

Acceptance allows us to be aware of the disease or dysfunction without letting it take us over. In acceptance, we can be surrounded by the disease of racism while choosing not to be part of it. Awareness of our power to choose gives us the freedom to excavate for truth in our own hearts. It is here where we become an outsider to the dysfunction, are able to see it with clear eyes, and be truthful about what we are seeing. It is here, as we step outside of the problem, where we become more observant and start making different choices.

As we listen, watch, or read about experiences that are different from our own, we need to pay attention to feelings and emotions as they arise and be present with our own fight or flight responses. Sitting quietly with our feelings is not easy, but when the cause of those feelings is unmasked, it represents one less button that can be pushed within us, one less active trigger. It means the dagger that was keeping us from healing has been pulled out, and our wound finally has an opportunity to heal. Our healing frees vast amounts of energy that can help us on our way to the next level in our journey of transformation.

Acceptance is where I came to terms with the reality things are as they had been from ages past, but they did not have to stay the same.

This is where we begin to peel the layers of conditioning faster and more deliberately. It is where we come to terms with the power that lives within us. This is the stage where we see racism everywhere. We start to understand at a deeper level the ways in which racism hurts humanity in general, and Black people and People of Color in particular. It's where we see our connection to the pain of racism regardless of the color of our skin. Acceptance is a powerful step toward healing and a lead-in to the next stage in the process—reengagement.

QUESTIONS TO CONSIDER:

- What does acceptance mean to you?

- How do you do acceptance?

- How has your understanding of racism changed through this reading?

- Do you accept we have been racially conditioned?

CHAPTER 27

STAGE 8

REENGAGEMENT

———

"The world may not have changed, but I have."

—MILAGROS PHILLIPS

Reengagement happens after you've come to a place of acceptance and understand race and racism differently than you had in the past. Reengagement says, *"I've had an experience or lived through a process; I've changed, but the world hasn't. How will I engage with my world now?"*

As you can see, there are many dimensions of race and racism at play stemming from a caste system that was established hundreds of years ago. It's been passed down through the generations and still affects us today. You are no longer in a place of ignorance, but what about the people around you? You still have to engage with the toxicity out there. Remember where you were when you started this journey. The people in your life may not know what you now do. You are still living under the same racial caste, but you have changed. So how do you engage with the same old world in a whole new way?

At this point, you can reengage with race the way you've always engaged with it, or you can choose differently because you've just walked through a process that gives you information you can now use to understand your own filters and the filters of others. As you look around you, you notice some people are moving out of their denial state while others are still in denial. They say things like, *"I'm a good person; I don't see color."* And there are a lot of people who are in anger. We see it in the eruption that happens in protests around the world. Some people are bargaining with how they will engage with racism in their organizations and communities. They say things like, *"We will just treat all of our employees equally,"* while professing a culture of equity. They don't seem to understand equity is not equality. After centuries of White advantage, equity is about leveling the playing field.

Imagine a teeter-totter. On one side is a White person who grew up poor. Let's call him Jack. Jack managed to go to college, and when he graduated, he got a good-paying job with the ability to move up in the company. He is being mentored by a high-visibility, C-suite executive, and he is being groomed for success. They both have a lot in common, as they come from similar backgrounds. Yes, they both grew up poor, but both their parents owned their own homes. They were both hired at good salaries that allowed them to pay off their student loans, and when it came time to buy a home, the bank had no problem giving them a mortgage. Imagine those simple advantages as gold bars that add up on the tee-ter-totter. They both work hard, but their hard work pays off in promotions and salary hikes.

Now imagine a Black person on the other side of the teeter-totter. His name is Okwan. He also grew up poor and managed to go to college. He was told by his family and the media that education was the way out of poverty. Okwan and Jack work for the same company, do the same job, and were hired at the same time. But Okwan was hired at a much-reduced salary. It's difficult for him to help his family, take care of his personal expenses, and pay for his student loan on his current salary. So, he takes a second job. There is no one to mentor him in the company. At times, he's exhausted from holding two jobs, so his performance suffers. Most of the money from his second job goes to taxes, so he's still struggling. There are no bars of gold on Okwan's side of the teeter-totter. There are times when he feels hopeless, depressed, and exhausted.

Reengagement is the stage where we realize we can't engage with the world in the same way. Reengagement can be daunting and scary. It can leave us confused as to what to do next. The best way to manage reengagement is to take the time to process what you have learned.

The reengagement stage is a powerful stage. It is the stage where you realize you now have new and different information so you can make different decisions.

QUESTIONS TO CONSIDER:

- Equity is about balance. What needs to happen in the world, in organizations, and in communities for real equity to be present?

- How were you engaging with racism before you knew what you now know?

- How will you reengage race and racism now?

- Who do you need to forgive?

- Who needs to forgive you?

CHAPTER 28

STAGE 9
FORGIVENESS

———

RELEASE WITHOUT BLAME

*"For me, forgiveness and compassion are always linked:
how do we hold people accountable for wrongdoing and
yet at the same time remain in touch with their humanity
enough to believe in their capacity to be transformed?"*

—BELL HOOKS

Forgiveness is a charged word when it comes to the myth of race
and the daily violence of racism. How can we ever ask people
who for centuries have been robbed, violated, and continue to
be to forgive? It is a daring request! For many, forgiveness is
perceived as a way of allowing perpetrators to get away with
the wrong they have done. But nothing could be further from
the truth. Forgiveness is not for the perpetrators; forgiveness is
for the release of the victim. Forgiveness can prompt us to act
differently, breaking the cycle of violence that keeps us trapped.

For many, forgiveness itself is a journey that starts with, "*I will never forgive that!*" It takes us to, "*Maybe someday I'll be able to forgive.*" And if we continue on the path of healing, we get to, "*Someday I'll forgive, but I won't forget.*" However, true forgiveness comes with a kind of forgetting. When we reach true forgiveness, what one could previously not forgive no longer runs our lives. It stops being top of mind awareness and allows us to be free. Forgiveness releases those who have been wronged from carrying the guilt and shame of their perpetrator.

The perpetrator's cycle is different. Their cycle requires admission of the wrong, the need to make amends, reparations, a request for forgiveness, and ultimately to forgive the self for the wrong done to others. Forgiveness can be liberating for both victim and perpetrator, but when it comes to race and racism, that is a tall order. Consider many White people are unconscious of their racial conditioning, and People of Color are still living under an oppressive system that often threatens their lives. How could one fathom forgiveness in such a racially charged environment? On the other hand, what would it mean if we could forgive? What would it be like to release without blame?

Think back to some of the stories in this book, stories like the woman whose grandparents would not let her invite her kindergarten friend to her birthday party. Her grandparents were, in their own way, trying to keep her safe. Think of the unresolved pain of the child she never spoke with again. Think of my friend, the tennis club, and the woman who said if they had had access to the resources, they would have fixed the club for their children. While they were all responsible for their actions, reactions, and interactions, they were all acting out of the racial conditioning they received from the culture. Choosing forgiveness is not releasing them from accountability for their actions; it's about releasing you from carrying the burden of another's behavior. Forgiveness allows grace to flow and creates peace in the body and mind of the person who forgives. In some cases, forgiveness stops the cycle of violence.

I attended a conference on Women Waging Peace at the Kennedy School at Harvard many years ago. I have never thought of myself as a peacemaker until I was invited to that conference. There were women from various parts of the world. A young woman from Rwanda shared her mother had watched her husband be brutally murdered before her very eyes by four men during their 1994 Civil War. When the case came to trial in the Gacaca court, her mother testified and was asked what she wanted done with the four men. She asked they be released. She said when her husband was killed, she was left widowed, and her children were left without their father. She didn't want to have on her conscience the death of four men, their widows, and orphan children. She said she had forgiven them and wanted them to be released. Since the offended party had the right to choose what would happen with their assailant, the men were released. What she wanted was for the men and their families to gather with her family once a year to celebrate her husband's life.

But the story did not end there. The young woman said these men got jobs and helped her mother raise her and her siblings, allowing her to get an education and work for peace. She also spoke about how her mother's choice stopped the cycle of violence between their families, as the children of those men might have sought vengeance upon her and her siblings had her mother chosen to have them killed.

Forgiveness can be a powerful antidote to violence. Forgiveness takes courage and faith, and it is not dependent on the actions of the assailant. Forgiveness is about personal choice. Forgiveness enhances our transformation. Forgiveness marks a turning point in the healing process. Forgiveness allows us to show up in the world differently. It brings us back to center and adjusts for balance. Our willingness to forgive determines how we will move into the next stage of the healing process.

QUESTIONS TO CONSIDER:

- Have you ever forgiven anyone?

- When it comes to racism, is forgiveness possible?

- Is it possible to forgive while remaining in a toxic environment?

- What needs to happen for you to get to a place of forgiveness?

- Who do you need to forgive?

- Who needs to forgive you?

BECOMING EMPOWERED

"The process of spotting fear and refusing to obey it is the source of all true empowerment."
—MARTHA BECK

CHAPTER 29

STAGE 10

WITNESSING

———

*"He who fights with monsters might take care
lest he thereby become a monster."*

—FRIEDRICH NIETZSCHE

In the process of racial healing, witnessing is more than just telling or listening to the story. Witnessing is about how we show up in the world. Witnessing is about the choices we make in the moment and whether we choose to act, react, and interact with others from power or powerlessness. Let's define power because power is one of those misconstrued words that throw us off. Here is a story that helps us define power and powerlessness.

I was attending a graduation at the School of Education at the University of Massachusetts Amherst in the late 1990s. The keynote speaker was an African-American man who was a triple-PhD physicist, we will call him Dr. Jones. He shared a story about something that happened to him, which was something that happened to several prominent Black men he knew, and more than one of them had had the same reaction as he did. Having just delivered a keynote speech for an international group of scientists in Geneva, he was standing in the lobby of a hotel waiting for his ride to the airport. An older White man walked up to him, handed him a set of keys, and asked him to get him his car. Dr. Jones had had this happen to him before, but this time, feeling sick and tired of White people assuming he was there to serve them, he decided to do something different. He just stood there, holding the man's keys. The man gave him a quizzical look like, *"Aren't you going to get my car?"* when a limousine pulled up to the door of the hotel. Dr. Jones walked out of the hotel, still holding the man's keys. The limo driver opened the door, Dr. Jones got in, and the limo pulled away. A few blocks away, he asked the driver to stop close to the trash can on the corner. He rolled down the window and threw away the man's keys.

I have shared that story in my seminar many times, and I asked the group, *"Where was Dr. Jones witnessing from, power, or powerlessness?"* Most people respond Dr. Jones was witnessing from power. Was he? To answer that question, we want to go back and look at our emotions chart of "love" and "fear," then we have to ask ourselves where power and powerlessness fall. Power is about love. Love is about connection, generosity, and compassion. No one can fault Dr. Jones for his actions. In this story, he was telling the Black students and Students of Color no matter how much education you get, there are people in this world who will always see you as their servant because of the color of your skin. At the same time, his actions came from a place of frustration and of recognizing a White person with a prison record can get a job easier than a Black college student with no police record.

He was reminding students racism is real and it will likely affect them negatively all their lives. It's a sad reality to send students out into the world with, but it is real.

While we can certainly understand Dr. Jones's frustration, it doesn't change the fact he was acting out of his pain and not his power. Dr. Jones is not responsible for educating White folks or helping them see the perceptions that come out of their conditioning. Power comes from seeing the dysfunction and not choosing to collude with it by creating more pain and feeding the dysfunction. At some point, witnessing is about choosing whether we will feed love or if we will continue to feed fear.

Witnessing is about telling our story. In the Black church, people go up to the pulpit to give witness, which is to tell their story to the rest of the congregation. In the case of the healing process, witnessing is also about how we treat ourselves and others.

QUESTIONS TO CONSIDER:

- When it comes to racism, where do you usually witness from, love or fear?

- Where do the people in your immediate family witness from?

- How do you feel in your body when you witness from fear?

- How do you feel in your body when you witness from love?

CHAPTER 30

STAGE 11
PROCESSING

———

*"The most powerful political voices are those
with a different way of seeing and processing the
world and the sounds that emanate from it."*

—SAUL WILLIAMS

We have traversed a lot of ground. At this stage, processing is integral to racial healing. In this context, processing is taking in as much of the information as we can and allowing it to move through us. This may bring up memories long forgotten, and it can bring up emotions. The processing stage is where we connect the dots, put things in perspective, and we begin to formulate a vision that is both individual and collective. It's in this stage we begin to look at our role as dictated by our systems and whether we fit those roles. Processing is about absorbing what has been learned and assessing how the new information fits into our lives and how it adds to our understanding. It's where we assess the damage done to ourselves and others, and we look at what's left. Processing is about allowing the information to move from the head to the heart, and finally to gut-level knowing, where it becomes part of our inner wisdom

This is the stage where one decides if one will interact with and be a witness to the world from a new perspective. Processing is the stage where we decide if we will give in to the pain and rage that has come up through this new awareness or choose love. Processing our anger is different than processing from anger. Whether we are aware of it or not, as we read through, we process every stage. As we read, we look at our own ignorance, innocence, and denial. We grieve the loss of our old self, the one who didn't really understand what racism was and believed the myth of race to be true. We grieve a world lost for centuries to dysfunction that has caused and continues to cause the loss of countless lives.

In his 2008 article in *Simple Psychology*, "Information Processing," Saul McLeod describes it this way: "*The information processing approach characterizes thinking as the environment providing input of data, which is then transformed by our senses. The information can be stored, retrieved, and transformed using 'mental programs,' with the results being behavioral responses.*"

Processing can take us minutes, hours, weeks, or months depending on the depth of the wound and our agency in treating it. This is where self-compassion and patience are vital to creating new ways of being. The Healer's Code is an opportunity to learn from the past, understand our racial conditioning, and create new ways of being and dealing with race and racism.

QUESTIONS TO CONSIDER:

- As you look back to where you were before you read this book in your awareness of racial conditioning, what was most difficult for you?

- What is new?

- What did you already know?

- Who are you as a result of looking at race through these new filters?

- What will you do now that you know what you know?

- Do you have a new vision, or are you still processing it?

- Are you feeling overwhelmed?

- Do you wish you could go back to sleep?

  In the next chapter, we will put this all together.

CHAPTER 31

STAGE 12
VISION

———

"Vision is the art of seeing what is invisible to others."

—JONATHAN SWIFT

Who are we without our visions, hopes, and dreams? It is
said without a picture of our desired outcome, we, the people, perish. A vision can draw us toward our future or stop
us dead in our tracks, and when it comes to race, we can't
afford to stop. Now is the time, and we are the ones who can
change this. What we create today will be the legacy we leave
for future generations. What kind of a world will you leave
for generations to come?

THIS IS THE CHAPTER YOU WRITE

Think of the journey you have taken as you read this book,
ask yourself the following questions, and write the answers in
a journal. Take the time to create a vision. Write this chapter
as if at the end of your life, you were looking back to a dream
come true, a vision you saw, a world you created. Write it

and then take action. You have all the tools. If you've come this far in the book, you have cracked the Healer's Code. Sit quietly, open your heart, then write your vision.

QUESTIONS TO CONSIDER:

- What kind of world do I want to leave behind?

- What will you contribute to the healing of racism?

- Who would we be as a human family without the legacy of the Doctrine of Discovery?

- What do you see as a possible future for us all?

- How does the new vision make you feel?

- How do you feel in your body?

CHAPTER 32

STAGE 13
TAKING ACTION

————

WHAT WILL YOU DO
TODAY TO CHANGE OUR
COLLECTIVE TOMORROW?

*"Vision without action is merely a dream. Action
without vision just passes the time. Vision
with action can change the world."*

—JOEL A. BARKER

Nothing awakens the spirit and takes us out of victim
mode like taking action. And not just taking action for
the sake of action but taking the right action. When we
do something to change our situation, it's as if life begins
to move toward us. Taking action will look different for
everyone reading this book. Not all of us are here to be
activists, but everyone can do something to change their
racial conditioning.

You'll know when you're taking the right action because you will feel right in your body. My suggestion in taking action is you first become race literate. The thing about race is everyone can do something. Here is a short-list of actions you can take to get you started thinking about what you can do, and to keep you racially awake and racially sober:

- Learn about the racial history of our nation

- Read more books about race and racism

- Buy from and support Black businesses

- Hold politicians accountable for the racist things they say and do

- Look at how your company's policies and procedures may be racist

- Hold a company, county, and national equity audit

- Help us create a national race literacy campaign

- Ask that health care providers and medical schools become racial-trauma informed and race literate

- See to it the educators in your schools are race literate

- Make sure your public servants are race literate

- See to it your favorite sports team becomes race literate

- Maintain an open mind about race

- Keep your heart open

- Engage with compassion

- Speak about race from your heart

- Create friendships with those who have a different life experience from you

- Pay equitable wages

- Speak up when something is wrong

- Think before you call the police on someone who is not harming you

There is something you can do to take positive action right where you are on this very day.

QUESTIONS TO CONSIDER:

- How will you take action?

- What can you do today to change your racial conditioning?

CHAPTER 33

CONNECTING THE DOTS

———

"You must learn to reason!"

—FELICIANO HUGHES WALTERS

My parents were amazing teachers! The things they said to me throughout my childhood still ring in my ears and become a guiding light whenever I feel lost as an adult. Like a mantra, my father would repeat, *"You must learn to reason!"* When I was a child, my father would insist I see the connection between things and that I "reason" things out. In a way, my parents' guidance helped me put this book together. My intuitive guidance led me to specific books and teachings.

My father was a techie from way back. He taught me you never get your news from just one place. When I was a child, we used to call my father the human antenna. He would listen to the local news in the Dominican Republic on his newest radio, but his old radio was tuned to the British Broadcasting Company (BBC). He had another radio tuned to Spain. Sometimes he would stand in the living room holding the wire to the radio, moving around the room to get the best reception the way some of us do with our cell phones when we can't get reception. It was from him and my mother's respect for the ancestors I learned life is not random and all things are connected.

Life is a continuum, and while each moment holds a new expression, every present moment holds a connection to the past. The simplicity and complexity of each moment holds the promise of a new beginning. Each moment is simple because it simply is. Each moment is complex because it's inextricably linked to the past. But each moment holds a promise of renewal and an opportunity for a new choice. We are only stuck in the past when we refuse to acknowledge it and therefore change it. The past hangs around like a small child pulling on their mother's dress, asking to be seen, to be recognized. Our racial past haunts every moment of every day, asking to be noticed, considered, and accepted.

Our racial history gives us context, deepens our understanding, and can help us see clearly. History helps us make sense of the senseless; it helps us understand behaviors and ways of communicating. The stages of healing help us see where we are in the process of transformation. They help us assess the places where we get triggered or stuck. They give us a vision and places we can move to.

Healing reminds us we are whole, that there are things that have happened to us as a species that have traumatized and broken us, yet here we still are. Healing helps us see our connection to ourselves and others. Healing peels away the layers of internalized racial conditioning, allowing us to find our power and use it in service to humanity. It frees up energy so we can create a new way of being. It helps us see the light in people, even when they can't see it in themselves.

Healing leads to empowerment and liberation. It helps us see how the wound and the salve live in the same place—within us. Healing our racial wounds takes us out of blame and shame and puts us in the driver's seat of our lives. It allows us to become a living bridge, connecting the past and the present. Healing helps us create space for a new future, leaving knowledge and wisdom for generations to come.

Healing may not be the easiest road to take, but if we allow it, it can be the most rewarding as we take action that leads to a new life. We are the generation that makes changes that affect the next generation. Think of what the Doctrine of Discovery has meant to humanity. What if we are the generation that is here to create a Doctrine of Equity, a Doctrine of Love? It is said we are the ones we have been waiting for. If that is true, we can no longer afford to wait.

Humans are extraordinary beings capable of great mayhem and great heights. Who would we be without the poison of racism? What would we create in unity, collaboration, and connection? What kind of a world would we bring forth if we allowed ourselves to dream?

The Healer's Code lays out a blueprint with some of the missing pieces to the puzzle. It lands us in the reality of our collective racial conditioning and gives us a way forward. May the Healer's Code serve as a way to re-member, a way to reconnect the human family.

CHAPTER 34

THE PRESCRIPTION

---

*"We cannot solve our problems with the same
thinking we used when we created them."*

—ALBERT EINSTEIN

Looking at our history, we realize the mind that created the Doctrine of Discovery was a sick, twisted mind acting out of greed, unresolved trauma, and a belief in "not enough." This is not to excuse, but to understand if we continue to live with the same mindset, no matter what we think we are creating, we're doing it with the same energy, and thereby recreating the past. The idea of not enough has ruled the world, so human beings believe they are not enough.

On the micro—the personal level—the idea we are "not enough" hovers around not tall enough, pretty enough, dark enough, light enough, rich enough, influential enough, and on and on and on. At the macro, the thinking is we are not enough to change the world, we are too small to make a difference, and that thinking is dangerous. That thinking not only got us here, but it also keeps us trapped in the problem. This is why understanding the history that got us to where we are is so important!

We crack the Healer's Code through our understanding, connecting the dots, and getting a more holistic view of the problem.

We crack the Healer's Code by seeing life as a continuum that moves from day to day, year to year, decade to decade, and generation to generation.

We crack the Healer's Code by realizing nothing is random; everything, every place, and everyone has a history; and we are inextricably linked to that history by the powerful thread that is life.

We crack the Healer's Code by creating a strategy that strengthens our belief in our wholeness, and we practice it until we can see who we really are; until we see nothing has altered the truth that lives within us; until we see the reason we have resilience is because we, in spite of all we have lived through, are still whole. It is from that wholeness our resilience comes.

In many ways, this book is the prescription for healing our racial conditioning and finding wholeness. Read it more than once. Share it. Talk about it.

The prescription is as easy as 1-2-3:

1. HISTORY

- Become race literate.

- Look to the past to understand the present.

- Debunk the myth of race.

2. UNDERSTANDING

- Understand we have been racially conditioned through hundreds of years of physical, emotional, and mental violence.

- Use the Healer's Code to understand where you, your family, your company, your community, or your country are in the process of healing. Remember we all absorbed the conditioning, depending on where we fall in the caste system; therefore, we all need healing.

- Be compassionate. People don't know what they don't know.

- Be patient, but don't be silent. Do your best to make a difference. Sometimes all we can do is plant seeds.

- While some may use words such as racist as a character judgment, based on dichotomous thinking, racism is about conditioning. We need to start treating racism as a condition that needs to be treated and healed.

3. DO SOMETHING

- Insist on the facts. You can't heal on a lie. Remember the misinformed are bound to miscreate.

- You are the only one who can change you.

- Remember you are whole, and you are enough!

- Remember who you are!

CHAPTER 35

PRACTICES TO SUPPORT YOUR HEALING

———

This segment is dedicated to supporting you in creating a practice of peace and wellbeing. These are suggestions that have worked for my students over time.

TAKE A LOVE SHOWER AM & PM

Before you go to sleep at night and when you wake up in the morning, imagine there is a beautiful light made of soft pastel colors, white, and gold about three hundred feet above your head. Let the light gently bathe you and fill you with love. Let the light flow in you and around you. Let it enter your cranium and fill your skull, your spine, and the front of your body. Let it flow out of the bottom of your spine and out of your feet down to the center of the Earth. Imagine the light anchoring you to the Earth by establishing roots. Now allow those roots to nourish you with the Earth's strength as it flows back into your body and out the top of your head. At night, allow this flow to lull you to sleep. In the morning, allow the Earth's strength to awaken your body. Take a few moments to flow this beautiful energy into your day and *breathe*!

NATURE

If you have a park nearby, go for a walk. If you have a tree on your street, stand underneath it, or just look up at the sky. Breathe deeply. Inhale slowly as if you were taking in the entire Earth. Exhale as if you were emptying your past. Do this five to ten times.

TAKE IN THE SOIL

Sit on the grass or the soil. Put your hands flat on the ground and imagine you are taking in the Earth. Let the energy from the ground enter your body through your pelvic floor and your hands. Imagine you are inhaling air coming up from the ground, filling your body, going out through the top of your head, and falling back down like a fountain.

DISCOVER NATURE'S JEWELS

Get a magnifying glass or a jeweler's loop. You can find them on the Web for just a few dollars. Go out into nature and use the jeweler's loop to look closely at leaves, stems, and flowers. Notice how everything shimmers. Look at the details and take in the colors. It's like magic!

NATURE ON TV

Trade one of your TV shows for a nature video with soft music.

SKIP FOR JOY

Go skipping with a friend. Hold hands while you skip and try not to laugh.

GRATITUDE

Practice gratitude with every breath. Be in appreciation for every breath you take. Thank your body for all the ways it serves you, how it takes you from one place to another. Offer gratitude for all your senses, one by one—touch, smell, taste, vision, hearing, and intuition.

WORD MEDITATIONS

Meditate on words that change your consciousness, such as peace, joy, appreciation, love, strength, beauty, and wealth. Word meditations also work great as walking meditations.

BREATHE

Traumatic and painful experiences often take our breath away, and not in a good way. Here are some breathing techniques I taught my sound therapy students in the 1990s. They are timeless and still produce the same results: a sense of peace and often a blissful state.

- Breathe deep into the diaphragm. Imagine you are filling up a bottle. You fill from the bottom up. Place your hands on your lower belly to feel the breath as it fills your body. Imagine the air as weighty and allow gravity to pull the breath down deep into the bottom of your diaphragm. Keep filling until your chest gets full. Hold for three seconds, longer if you can, and exhale slowly. Repeat five to ten times.

- As you sing "Ah" out loud, allow the breath to be released slowly, letting the sound out using as little air as possible. This will allow you to hold the note longer. This sound can be done sitting, but standing is best to experience the fullness of the sound. Repeat the exercise going through all the vowels—A, E, I, O, U—one at a time. Notice how you feel when you are done.

- Take five long, slow, deep breaths. Bring your focus to the center of your chest. Imagine a bright light shining in the center of your chest. In the center of the light is written the word "peace." Inhale and exhale while imagining the air is inhaled into the light and exhaled out of the light.

- Take a deep breath and imagine you are inhaling from every pore in your body. Exhale through every pore in your body. Exhale fast, as if you were exploding from the inside out. Repeat three to five times. Notice the energy coursing through your body.

- Take fast breaths for quick energy. Inhale through your nose and exhale through your mouth. As you inhale, push your belly out. As you exhale, pull your belly in. Start with ten of these breaths and build up to thirty or more. When you stop, feel the energy in your body.

Try some of these exercises and find one or two that work to keep you calm and at peace. Get used to them. This way, you have some calming exercises you can use next time you're involved in a difficult situation, especially one involving race.

APPENDIX

―――

INTRODUCTION

Phillips, Milagros. *11 Reasons to Become Race Literate*. Milagros A. Phillips. May 16, 2016.

PART 1

CHAPTER 1

Chan, Master Luke. *101 Miracles of Natural Healing with Master Luke Chan*. Benefactor Press. VHS.

CHAPTER 2

Castañón, Laura. "Everything the Human Body Does is Guided by Chemistry We Don't Fully Understand. Yet." Northwestern University. October 10, 2018. https://news.northeastern.edu/2018/10/10/everything-the-human-body-does-is-guided-by-chemistry-we-dont-fully-understand-yet/.

Cohen, Elizabeth. *CDC: Antidepressants most prescribed drugs in US*. CNN. July 9, 2007. https://www.cnn.com/2007/HEALTH/07/09/antidepressants/#cnnSTCVideo.

Empower Work Team. "What is Imposter Syndrome." *Empower Work*. 2021. https://www.empowerwork.org/blog/work-issue-101-imposter-syndrome.

Lieberman, Matthew. *Social: Why our brains are wired to connect*. OUP Oxford. October 8, 2013.

McPhillips, Deidre. "US 3rd Most Depressed Country According to the World Health Organization." *US News*. September 14, 2016. https://www.usnews.com/news/best-countries/articles/2016-09-14/the-10-most-depressed-countries.

CHAPTER 3

Culver, Jordan. "Racism Public Health Issue." *USA Today*. November 24, 2020. https://www.usatoday.com/story/news/nation/2020/11/23/racism-public-health-issue-145-us-places-now-work-begins/6385693002/.

Degruy, Dr. Joy. "Post Traumatic Slave Syndrome." Joy De Gruy. 2021.
https://www.joydegruy.com/post-traumatic-slave-syndrome.

Holland, Kimberly. "What is Stockholm Syndrome and Who Does it
Affect?" Healthline. November 11, 2019.
https://www.healthline.com/health/mental-health/stockholm-syndrome#definition.

Li, David K. "Former Minneapolis Police Officer Derek Chauvin to be Tried
Separately in George Floyd Death Case." *NBC News*. January 12, 2021.
https://www.nbcnews.com/news/us-news/former-minneapolis-police-officer-derek-
chauvin-be-tried-separately-george-n1253905.

Liu, Marian. "Skin Whiteners Are Still in Demand, Despite Health Concerns" *CNN
Health*. September 2, 2018.
https://www.cnn.com/2018/09/02/health/skin-whitening-lightening-asia-intl/index.html.

Oxford Online Dictionary. s.v. "Colonization." (n.) Accessed June 23, 2021.
https://www.oxfordlearnersdictionaries.com/definition/english/
colonization?q=colonization.

CHAPTER 5

Nichols, Dr. Edwin. "Axiology." *Afrometaphysics*. March 2015.
http://www.afrometaphysics.org/wp-content/uploads/2015/03/Cultural-Differences-
Chart.pdf.

The Tonight Show Starring Jimmy Fallon. "Jane Elliott on Her 'Blue Eyes/Brown Eyes
Exercise' and Fighting Racism." June 2, 2020. YouTube Video, 7:16.
https://www.youtube.com/watch?v=f2z-ahJ4uws.

Women's History Month. "Female Warriors in the Middle Ages 5th to 14th
Centuries." 2021.
https://womenshistorymonth.wordpress.com/resources/women-and-series/women-
and-war/female-warriors/.

CHAPTER 6

Eskeon, Jamie. "What is Stockholm Syndrome." *Medical News Today*. October 1, 2020.
https://www.medicalnewstoday.com/articles/stockholm-syndrome#what-it-is.

Kounang, Nadia. "What Is the Science Behind Fear?" *CNN Health*. October 29. 2015.
https://www.cnn.com/2015/10/29/health/science-of-fear/index.html.

CHAPTER 7

Kreisman, Daniel and Marcos A. Rangel. "On the Blurring of the Color Line: Wages
and Employment for Black Males of Different Skin Tones." *The Review of Economics
and Statistics*. March 2015. MIT Press Direct, Volume 97 Issue 1.
https://direct.mit.edu/rest/issue/97/1.

Meeri, Kim. "Study Finds That Fear Can Travel Quickly Through Generations of
Mice." *Washington Post*. Health & Science. December 7, 2013.
https://www.washingtonpost.com/national/health-science/study-finds-that-fear-
can-travel-quickly-through-generations-of-mice-dna/2013/12/07/94dc97f2-5e8e-
11e3-bc56-c6ca94801fac_story.html.

Merriam-Webster Online Dictionary. s.v. "Definition of Trauma." (n.) 2021. Accessed 6/23/2021.
https://www.merriam-webster.com/dictionary/trauma.

Quigley, Narda, Srikant Devaraj, and Pankaj C. Patel. "The Effects of Skin Tone, Height, and Gender on Earnings," *PLoS ONE 13(1): e0190640.* January 2, 2018.
https://doi.org/10.1371/journal.pone.0190640.

Yehuda, Rachel. "The Trauma of Slavery is Encoded in the Genes of Black People." *Atlanta Star.* October 18, 2016. Youtube Video, 0:56.
https://www.youtube.com/watch?v=q8AX_qdxWVs.

CHAPTER 8

Biography.com Editors. "Henry the Navigator Biography." The Biography.com website. A&E Television Networks. Accessed 2020.
https://www.biography.com/explorer/henry-the-navigator.

Charles, Mark and Soong-Chan Rah. *Unsettling Truths: The Ongoing, Dehumanizing Legacy of the Doctrine of Discovery.* InterVarsity Press. November 5, 2019.

Menakem, Resmaa. "Generational Trauma." The Kiloby Center for Recovery. January 1, 2019. *YouTube Video,* 3:33.
https://www.youtube.com/watch?v=dk4PnbWIq_Q.

CHAPTER 9

Holland, Brynn. "The 'Father of Modern Gynecology' Performed Shocking Experiments on Enslaved Women." *History.* 2021.
https://www.history.com/news/the-father-of-modern-gynecology-performed-shocking-experiments-on-slaves.

Phillips, Milagros. *Speaking Race in Healthcare: A Manual for the Dialogue.* CreateSpace Independent Publishing Platform. December 13, 2018.

CHAPTER 10

History.com Editors. "Jim Crow Laws." *HISTORY.* Last updated March 26, 2021.
https://www.history.com/topics/early-20th-century-us/jim-crow-laws.

Lincoln, Abraham. "The Emancipation Proclamation." National Archives. Last reviewed on April 17, 2019. Accessed on June 23, 2021.
https://www.archives.gov/exhibits/featured-documents/emancipation-proclamation#:~:text=President%20Abraham%20Lincoln%20issued%20the,and%20henceforward%20shall%20be%20free.%22.

The District of Columbia Emancipation Act of 1862. "Reparation to Slave Owners." National Archives. Accessed June 23, 2021.
https://www.archives.gov/exhibits/featured-documents/dc-emancipation-act.

Sánchez, José Eduardo and Rebecca Fowler. "Closing the Race Gap." Young Invincibles. Published 2014.
https://younginvincibles.org/wp-content/uploads/2017/04/Closing_the_Race_Gap_TX-12.22.pdf.

CHAPTER 11

American Civil Liberties Union. "Marijuana Arrests by the Numbers." ACLU. Published 2021. https://www.aclu.org/gallery/marijuana-arrests-numbers.

Ingraham, Christopher. "White People Are More Likely to Deal Drugs, But Black People Are More Likely to Get Arrested for It." *Washington Post*. September 30, 2014. https://www.washingtonpost.com/news/wonk/wp/2014/09/30/white-people-are-more-likely-to-deal-drugs-but-black-people-are-more-likely-to-get-arrested-for-it/.

Langston, Abbie, Justin Scoggins, and Matthew Walsh. "Race and the Work of the Future: Advancing Workforce Equity in the United States." National Fund Org. November 12, 2020. https://nationalfund.org/learning-evaluation/publications/race-and-the-work-of-the-future/?gclid=CjwKCAiAgc-ABhA7EiwAjev-jo6hrSwXfsSZePmk9XHp9qumZn sqBl68evzTdJWXiEiftCRTHoL7NRoCaY4QAvD_BwE.

CHAPTER 13

Piddington, Director Andrew. *The Real Eve*. Scripts. 2021. Documentary. 103 mins. https://www.scripts.com/script/the_real_eve_21166.

CHAPTER 14

Adams, Susan. "White High School Drop-Outs Are as Likely to Land Jobs as Black College Students." *Forbes*. June 27, 2014. https://www.forbes.com/sites/susanadams/2014/06/27/white-high-school-drop-outs-are-as-likely-to-land-jobs-as-black-college-students/?sh=6dc960ac7b8f.

Gewertz, Ken. "Albert Einstein, Civil Rights Activist." *The Harvard Gazette*. April 12, 2007. *https://news.harvard.edu/gazette/story/2007/04/albert-einstein-civil-rights-activist/*.

McMillan, Rob. "Upland School Calls Police on 5-Year-Old Boy ." *ABC7*. March 1, 2019. https://abc7.com/upland-elementary-school-cops-called-on-kid-kindergartener-has-him-police-kindergarten-student/5161897/.

Oxford Language Dictionary. s.v. "Colonization." (n.) Accessed June 24, 2021. https://www.google.com/search?q=what+is+colonization&oq=What+is+colonization&aqs=chrome.0.0i433j0l9.9189j1j7&sourceid=chrome&ie=UTF-8.

CHAPTER 15

Findley, Elisha and Emma McElligott. "A Reaction to Slave Music." Accessed June 23, 2021. http://41114544.weebly.com/follow-the-drinking-gourd.html.

PART 2

CHAPTER 16

Paul, Sheryl. "The Cycle of Healing." *Huffington Post*. July 2020. https://www.huffpost.com/entry/the-cycle-of-healing_b_11081788#:~:text=We%20learn%20and%20heal%20in,where%20peace%20and%20clarity%20reside.

CHAPTER 17

McCraty, Rollin. "The Role of the Heart in Healing Racism." HeartMath Institute. 2021. https://www.heartmath.org/about-us/team/founder-and-executives/.

CHAPTER 19

Merriam-Webster Dictionary. s.v. "Innocence." (n.) Accessed July 2, 2021. https://www.merriam-webster.com/dictionary/innocence.

Riddle, Travis and Stacey Sinclair. "Racial Disparities in School-Based Disciplinary Actions Are Associated with County-Level Rates of Racial Bias." PNAS. April 2, 2019. https://www.pnas.org/content/116/17/8255.

CHAPTER 25

McPhillips, Deidre. "U.S. Among Most Depressed Countries in the World China Leads In Various Categories Tracked by the World Health Organization." *US News.* September 14, 2016. https://www.usnews.com/news/best-countries/articles/2016-09-14/the-10-most-depressed-countries.

CHAPTER 29

McLeod, Saul. "Information Processing." *Simple Psychology.* 2008. https://www.simplypsychology.org/information-processing.html.

SUGGESTED READING

Cook, Gareth. "Why We are Wired for Connection." *Scientific American.* October 22, 2013. https://www.scientificamerican.com/article/why-we-are-wired-to-connect/.

DiAngelo, Dr. Robin. "Why It's So Hard for a White to Talk About Racism." July 3, 2018. YouTube video, https://www.youtube.com/watch?v=45ey4jgoxeU.

"Energetic Communication." In *Science of the Heart.* The HeartMath Institute. 2021. https://www.heartmath.org/research/science-of-the-heart/energetic-communication/.

Frazier, Edward Franklin. "The Pathology of Race." *Forum.* Originally published 1927.

Gruver, Jackson. "Racial Wage Gap for Men." Payscale. May 7, 2019. https://www.payscale.com/data/racial-wage-gap-for-men.

Holland, Kimberly. "Disastrous Doctrine Had Papal Roots." *National Catholic Reporter News.* November 11, 2019. https://www.ncronline.org/news/justice/disastrous-doctrine-had-papal-roots.

McPhillips, Deidre. "The 10 Most Depressed Countries." *USNews.* September 14, 2016. https://www.usnews.com/news/best-countries/articles/2016-09-14/the-10-most-depressed-countries.

Miller, Stephen. "Black Workers Still Earn Less than Their White Counterparts." SHRM. June 11, 2020. https://www.shrm.org/resourcesandtools/hr-topics/compensation/pages/racial-wage-gaps-persistence-poses-challenge.aspx.

Ryan, Joan. "Race Divides Our English into Dialects / White America Ignores a Major Language Factor." SFGate. January 28, 2012. https://www.sfgate.com/bayarea/article/Race-divides-our-English-into-dialects-White-2777600.php.

Stell, Alexander J. and Tom Farsides. "Brief Loving-Kindness Meditation Reduces Racial Bias, Mediated by Positive Other-Regarding Emotions." University of Sussex, Brighton, UK. Accepted for publication in Motivation and Emotions, 2015. https://www.researchgate.net/profile/Alexander_Stell/publication/282418631_Brief_loving-kindness_meditation_reduces_racial_bias_mediated_by_positive_other-regarding_emotions/links/562f745808ae0077ccc9a369/Brief-loving-kindness-meditation-reduces-racial-bias-mediated-by-positive-other-regarding-emotions.pdf.

ShuswapNation. Newcomb, Steven. "Our Original Free and Independent Existence as Nations and Peoples." Doctrine of Discovery. 2014. YouTube Video, 58:22. https://www.youtube.com/watch?v=0R-mR247akA.

The Berbers C. "10,000 BCE- Present Queen Candace of Kush C. 350 BCE." *Urban Intellectuals Black History Flashcards*. Volume 4 Pre 1492.

ABOUT THE AUTHOR

———

Milagros Phillips Keynote Speaker, TEDx Presenter, four times author, and certified coach. She specializes in creating space for engaging in difficult conversations. She designs strategic learning programs for clients seeking to enhance equity & inclusion (EI) by adding race literacy to their EI initiatives. Her programs use history, science, research, and storytelling to create compelling, life-transforming experiences that lead to understanding. With more than 35 years of experience in learning and development, Milagros consults, designs, and facilitates programs across many industries and services. Milagros is an artist/painter; she is the Producer/Host of Race Healer TV, the creator of Race Healer Magazine, and is fluent in English and Spanish.

To learn more about her work...
Visit: www.MilagrosPhillips.com
Email: info@milagrosphillips.com
Watch her TEDx: https://www.milagrosphillips.com/ted-x-talk

Her other books are:

- Speaking Race in Healthcare: A Manual for the Dialogue

- 8 Essentials to a Race Conversation & Manual to a New Dialogue

- 11 Reasons to Become Race Literate: A Pocket Guide to a New Conversation